Macmillan Studies in Religion

Christianity

A Living Faith

Macmillan Studies in Religion
Series editor: W. N. Greenwood

Christianity
A Living Faith

Barbara Wintersgill

MACMILLAN

To Charlotte, on the occasion of her baptism

© Barbara Wintersgill 1989

All rights reserved. No reproduction, copy or transmission
of this publication may be made without written permission.

No paragraph of this publication may be reproduced, copied
or transmitted save with written permission or in accordance
with the provisions of the Copyright Act 1956 (as amended),
or under the terms of any licence permitting limited copying
issued by the Copyright Licensing Agency, 33–4 Alfred Place,
London WC1E 7DP.

Any person who does any unauthorised act in relation to
this publication may be liable to criminal prosecution and
civil claims for damages.

First published 1989

Published by
MACMILLAN EDUCATION LTD
Houndmills, Basingstoke, Hampshire RG21 2XS
and London
Companies and representatives
throughout the world

Typeset by Wessex Typesetters
(Division of The Eastern Press Ltd)
Frome, Somerset

Printed in Hong Kong

British Library Cataloguing in Publication Data
Wintersgill, Barbara
Christianity.
1. Christianity – For schools
I. Title
200
ISBN 0–333–37644–7

Contents

Acknowledgements

The author and publishers wish to thank the following who have kindly given permission for the use of copyright material.

Board for Social Responsibility for extracts from 'Worth at Work' by David Eaton, *The Crucible*, July 1985;
Catholic Herald Ltd for 'Pilgrims of hope at the nuclear air bases' by Christopher Ralls, *Catholic Herald*, 27 April 1984;
Howard Elcock for extracts from a letter, *Guardian*, 1 May 1985;
John Gummer for extracts from 'What a bishop should not say', *Guardian*, 29 April 1985;
Hodder and Stoughton Ltd for extracts from *God's Smuggler* by Brother Andrew; *The Hiding Place* by Corrie ten Boom; and *Chasing the Dragon* by Jackie Pullinger with Andrew Quickie;
Paul Johns for extracts from 'Why we're campaigning this Easter', *Methodist Recorder*, 19 April 1984;
London Express News and Feature Services for 'Maggie's plea to the bishops' by Andrew Grice, *Daily Express*, 15 February 1988;
Ron Southey for extracts from a letter, *Guardian*, 1 May 1985.

The author and publishers wish to acknowledge the following photograph sources:

Amwell Studios pp. 2 right, 30 left, 37, 38, 47, 50 bottom; Andes Press Agency pp. 2 top, 2 left, 7, 10 top, 11, 19, 35, 41, 51, 53, 56, 65, 66, 78, 79, 81, 87, 96, 97, 99, 102, 103, 104, 105, 107 bottom, 110, 129, 131, 172, 183; BBC Hulton Picture Library p. 141; Cambridge Newspaper Ltd p. 85; Camera Press pp. 16, 21, 75, 154 top left; J. Allan Cash Limited pp. 153 top right, 154 bottom, 155 top; CAWTU p. 170; Colorsport pp. 29, 153 top left; The Guardian pp. 20, 179; Frank and Jane Haslam p. 49; John and Penny Hubley p. 157; Chris Kelly pp. 12, 30, top, 98, 101; Roman Kukiewicz pp. 108, 620; Mansell Collection p. 88; Methodist Home Mission pp. 10 bottom, 106, 107 top, 160, 173; National Film Archives p. 141; Picturepoint p. 31; Rex Features p. 74; Alan Race pp. 6, 109, 111; Dave Richardson p. 30 right; Slabbinck/Vanpoulles pp. 112, 113, 114; Morris Walker p. 50 top; Barbara Wintersgill pp. 89, 127.

The publishers have made every effort to trace the copyright holders, but where they have failed to do so they will be pleased to make the necessary arrangements at the first opportunity.

Cover photo: By kind permission of the Trustees of Sir Stanley Spencer Will Trust/City of Aberdeen Art Gallery.

Preface

Religious Education has undergone profound changes in the recent past. This series, *Macmillan Studies in Religion*, has been planned to take account of these changes with reference both to syllabus content and to those skills of learning which are now required of the student. While each book is independent of others in the series, the general approach adopted by the authors is similar. Each writer has in mind the student who is preparing for entry to public examinations in Religious Studies at 16+ and provision is made for students of a wide range of ability.

Each book, therefore, contains basic factual information together with 'extension material' which gives scope for work at a deeper level and/or further factual material for those who work more quickly. The text also incorporates 'stimulus material' to promote discussion and to foster the skills of understanding and evaluation; these skills are then applied by the student to written work in response to questions.

The approach which is characteristic of this series is one which is objective, fair and balanced. The reader is encouraged to consider a number of differing approaches to the subject matter and to respond to 'the challenging and varied nature of religion' (cf. Aim 2 of the National Criteria for Religious Studies, 1985). The first books to be published will bring new perspectives to bear on 'traditional' areas (the Synoptic Gospels and Social and Moral Issues) and to an area which features prominently in all recent syllabuses for 16+ examinations: 'Christianity'.

W. N. Greenwood
Series Editor

Foreword

Before beginning to work with this book, teachers should be aware of the following features:

1 *Objectives*. Each chapter begins with an analysis of the subject matter in relation to the assessment objectives of GCSE. It is hoped that this will assist both teachers and pupils in bearing those objectives in mind as they work.

2 *Coursework*. There are many suggestions for coursework in the book. The GCSE examining boards specify the three assessment objectives, Knowledge, Understanding, Evaluation, in different proportions. To assist pupils in putting together a coursework package which will satisfy the demands of their examining board, each individual item of coursework has been designated as K, U or E. It will be up to the teacher to allocate the relevant weighting to each item of work within a complete coursework assignment. (So that, for instance, pupils studying with LEAG will select only an item which covers *one* objective, and the teacher will allocate it a maximum of 20 marks.)

3 *Credo*. There is no one chapter dealing in isolation with Christian belief, although there is some summary work on this in the last chapter. Belief is investigated within the context of topics studied. The heading 'Credo' indicates that at this point certain key beliefs illustrated in the Creeds are being illustrated, and the relevant sections of the creeds are quoted.

4 *Resources*. No one book can, or indeed should, satisfy all the demands of a syllabus. Each chapter ends with a list of resources which should be available for pupils in a well-equipped classroom. One or two copies of each book should be adequate for reference. Remember to PLAN in advance. It may be that books, artefacts, and audio-visual aids need to be ordered from a central resources centre. It would be wise to book the resources you need well in advance.

1 The Christian family – then and now

Objectives for Chapter 1

1 What you should KNOW.
That Christianity is a worldwide religion; that Christians, while agreeing on many points of belief and moral code, differ in what they believe and how they practise their religion.

2 What you should UNDERSTAND.
(a) *New words and technical terms*
denomination; Reformation; evangelism; encyclical; *aggiornamento*; Catholic; Protestant
(b) *People, writings and traditions*
(i) Important people: e.g. Jesus; St Paul; Constantine; the Pope (NB John XXIII); Patriarch; Archbishop of Canterbury; Bishop; Priest; Minister.
(ii) Writings: The Bible.
(iii) Traditions: the major denominations of the Christian family (NB Roman Catholic, Orthodox, Anglican, the Protestant Churches. Also modern movements such as Taizé, Iona, the Second Vatican Council; The Ecumenical Movement; The World Council of Churches; Mission; Evangelism.
(c) *Belief*
The principal beliefs of Christianity expressed in the Apostles' and the Nicene creeds. The major differences in belief between Christians, especially regarding Apostolic Succession and the Priesthood of all Believers.
(d) *Questions about the meaning of life*
Can any religion, or any one group within a religious tradition, claim to teach 'the Truth'? Is Christianity the only means to salvation?

3 What you should be able to DO.
Evaluate, on the basis of evidence and argument, issues arising from the study of this chapter.

Talking pictures

These pictures all have something to do with being a Christian. In groups, see how much you can say about each picture. Ask yourselves what each picture has to do with Christianity. Share your ideas with the rest of the class

As you start on this chapter, you should realise that no single description can be applied to all Christians. Indeed, it would be quite wrong to talk about people of *any* religion as though they all believed and practised the same things. It is probably true to say that among Christians there are more differences than can be found within any other major world religion.

How it all began

The one thing which binds Christians together is that they are all followers of Jesus of Nazareth. Jesus was a Jew, born in Judaea almost 2000 years ago. We know about him from the New Testament, the writings of the Jewish historian Josephus, and from references to him in the writings of the Roman historians Tacitus, Suetonius and Pliny the Younger. Jesus was put to death by the Roman governor Pontius Pilate at the wish of Jewish leaders who were afraid that his teaching was causing a disturbance in the country. There then followed three stages in the growth of the 'church'.

1 On the third day after Jesus was crucified, some of his followers saw him alive again, and they began to teach that he had risen from the dead, and was the Son of God. Some of the Jewish people believed them and joined their group. In this way the Church began. Very soon, non-Jews (Gentiles) began to join.
2 In AD 1054 the churches of Eastern Europe separated from the church in the West. The Eastern churches were called the *Orthodox* churches and were centred largely in Russia, Greece and Armenia. The church in the West continued to be dominated by the Roman Church.
3 The third division occurred in the sixteenth century and is known as the *Reformation*. It only affected the Western church. Under the leadership of men like Martin Luther, John Calvin and John Knox, the *Protestant* Churches of Europe were set up. In England, Henry VIII rebelled against the authority of the Pope, called himself the Head of the Church in England, and so the Church of England was born. There is no one Protestant church. Many churches call themselves Protestant, such as the Baptists, United Reformed, Lutheran, Dutch Reformed, Church of Scotland. You will be coming across some of them during the course of this book.

At this stage, Christianity was still primarily the religion of Europe. From the sixteenth century onwards, and especially during the nineteenth century, Christian missionaries began to travel the world gaining new converts to the faith. Now in the twentieth century it is a religion which is practised in one form or another in almost every country in the world.

One faith – many faces

Today, there are more than 20 000 Christian groups. Some of them have millions of members, some have only a few In this book there is only the space to study the best-known groups, but if you are interested in finding out about some of the others, you can make this your own research task.

The various Christian groups and churches are often called *denominations*. This is a word which will be used throughout this book, and it is important that you remember what it means.

Research activity
Draw a family tree of the Christian Church, showing:
(a) the relationships between the main branches.
(b) the dates (approximately) at which each branch began.

Some statistics
It is very difficult to obtain precise numbers of Christians throughout the world. First, there is the question of exactly who to include – should statistics represent just those who attend church regularly, or a wider group? Also, in some countries people are very nervous of admitting that they are Christians, because Christianity is frowned upon by the government. However, the following statistics have been taken from the *World Christian Encyclopedia* (ed. D. B. Barrett) and represent figures for 1980.

Look at the tables.

Total world population – 5 billion (5,000,000,000)
Total Christian population – 1,425,924,589

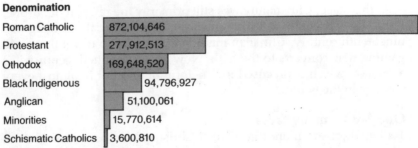

Location

Location	
Europe	420,926,340
S. America	392,204,600
Africa	236,278,850
N. America	227,237,570
S. Asia	125,914,645
Russia	107,168,000
E. Asia	22,324,690
Australasia	21,537,492

Denomination

Denomination	
Roman Catholic	872,104,646
Protestant	277,912,513
Othodox	169,648,520
Black Indigenous	94,796,927
Anglican	51,100,061
Minorities	15,770,614
Schismatic Catholics	3,600,810

Now answer these questions.

1 Which continent has
   (a) the highest
   (b) the second highest and
   (c) the third highest
   Christian population?

2 Why do you think that more Christians live in these three continents than in any of the others? (If you can't work it out, ask your History department for help!)

3 If you don't know the answer to this question—guess! What is the most commonly-spoken language among Christians? (The answer is at the bottom of p.27.)

4 List in descending order the three continents which have the smallest Christian populations.

5 Try to give reasons why fewer Christians live in these three continents.

6 Make a bar graph to show the distribution of Christians throughout the continents. (If you get stuck, ask the Maths department for help.)

Look at the tables on p.4.

1 Draw a pie chart to show the proportion of Christians belonging to each denomination. Don't forget to give a key.

2 What percentage of the world population is Christian? (to the nearest whole number)

3 What percentage of Christians are Roman Catholic? (to the nearest whole number)

4 What percentage of the world population is Roman Catholic? (to the nearest whole number)

The Orthodox Church

Like the Coptic and Jacobite churches, the Orthodox Church has changed very little over the centuries. This church keeps up very ancient traditions. If you look on a bookstall in an Orthodox Church, you will find that some of the most important writings are those of fourth- and fifth-century saints whose teachings are still, after the Bible, the foundation of the Orthodox faith. These are saints who are not heard of so commonly in the West – people like Basil, John Chrysostom, and Athanasius. The Orthodox Church has no leader like the Pope, although the *Ecumenical Patriarch of Constantinople* is particularly honoured. However, even he does not interfere in the affairs of other Churches. There are four especially ancient and honoured churches in the Orthodox family. These are the churches of Constantinople, Jerusalem, Antioch (Syria) and Jerusalem. Each of these churches is led by a *patriarch*. There are eleven other churches also led by a patriarch, archbishop or metropolitan. These are Albania, Bulgaria, Cyprus, Czechoslovakia, Georgia, Greece, Poland,

Pope John Paul II celebrates High Mass in St Peter's basilica, Rome.

power to forgive sins. (Matthew 18:18) They also were the ones who were with Jesus at the Last Supper, to whom he said 'do this in remembrance of me'. These were the twelve men who founded the first churches and led them.

As they grew old, they appointed other men to succeed them, called bishops, or presbyters. These men received their authority to teach the truth as they had heard it from the disciples. They were also given the authority to govern the churches. They in turn taught others and handed their authority on to them, and so on. This means that every bishop can, in theory, trace his succession back through the bishops who consecrated him to one of the apostles. It is regarded as very important that only a bishop, and the priests whom he ordains, may consecrate the bread and wine at the Eucharist. This is because when the words of consecration are said, God mysteriously acts through the priest in making the bread and wine become the body and blood of Christ.

The Roman Catholic Church points to a passage in Matthew 16:13–20, and claims that Jesus first gave the authority to bind and loose sins to St Peter, also calling Peter 'the Rock on whom I will build my Church'. Peter is said to have been the first Bishop of Rome, and just as Peter was the first among the apostles, so the Bishop of Rome, in succession to Peter, is the first among bishops.

In what ways do the men look alike?
In Russia, the Orthodox Church is still strong in many places, even though it is not supported by the government. Here, priests and deacons take part in the Easter procession, carrying the loaf of bread baked specially for the occasion.

Romania, Russia, Serbia and Sinai. There are also quite large Orthodox communities in Finland, China and Japan.

All Orthodox churches are self-governing. This means that they are independent and do not owe allegiance to anyone but their own archbishop or metropolitan. In spite of this, the different churches have remained united in belief and practice – although, not surprisingly, different traditions and customs have developed within national groups (e.g. at a Greek wedding the bride and groom have coronets of flowers placed on their heads, whereas in Russian churches crowns are used).

The Roman Catholic Church
The head of the Roman Catholic Church is the Bishop of Rome, more commonly called the *Pope* or 'Holy Father'.

One of the major differences between the Protestant churches on the one hand, and the Orthodox, Roman Catholic and Anglican (Church of England) churches on the other, is their belief about the priesthood.

Orthodox, Roman Catholic and Anglican churches argue that Jesus chose twelve men to be his special disciples, and that he gave them

The Second Vatican Council

In 1958 Cardinal Roncalli was elected pope at the age of 78. He took the name John XXIII, and although he only lived for another five years, will almost certainly be remembered as the best loved and most influential pope of the twentieth century.

It is said that none of the cardinals who elected him, and no one in the Curia (the group of priests, bishops and cardinals who run the Church from the Vatican), knew what sort of pope John XXIII would be. It was certainly a surprise to most Roman Catholics when in 1959 he announced that he was going to call a second Vatican Council (the first had begun in 1869 and declared the pope to be infallible in matters of doctrine).

The council opened in 1962 and was attended by every bishop in the world (unless too ill to come). The word which John made popular was *aggiornamento*, which means 'bringing up to date'. Many decisions were taken by the Council. Here are some of the most important:

1 Roman Catholic writers were to be allowed more freedom to publish books on Christian belief and the Church. After the Council, the books of the French priest Teilhard de Chardin were published and became bestsellers.

2 The council emphasised that *all* bishops had authority, not just the pope. The doctrine of papal infallibility still remained, but individual priests and bishops were given more authority over their churches, and the church as a whole.

3 Perhaps the changes which were most noticed by Catholic laymen were the liturgical changes. Until Vatican II, priests had said Mass with their backs to the people, and the service was usually whispered – quickly – in Latin, a language which few people understood. The council changed all this, and mass was now celebrated facing the people, in the language of the people, and in a tone of voice which could be heard.

4 The Council encouraged local churches to set up their own area councils, or meetings, of Roman Catholics. This too suggested that local priests and people were to be given more independence and freedom of thought.

5 Pope John set up a commission to advise on the issue of birth control. He did not live to hear its findings.

6 Roman Catholics were encouraged to take up a more friendly attitude to Christians of other denominations.

Although Vatican II was greeted with enthusiasm by millions of Christians of all denominations, there were inevitably some traditional Roman Catholics who did not approve of any sort of change. There were also some who were confused by the changes. For some people it was very unsettling to realise that some issues were being openly discussed which they thought left no room for argument – issues like birth control, euthanasia, abortion and the marriage of clergy.

Vatican II brought about enormous changes in the Roman Catholic Church, and it is a pity that for many people the council's contribution has been forgotten in the light of the decision which was eventually reached concerning family planning. John's commission on birth control reported back to his successor, the more conservative Paul VI The commission recommended that Roman Catholics *should* be allowed to use artificial methods of birth control, but Paul did not take their advice and issued a famous encyclical *Humanae Vitae* in 1968. (An encyclical is a letter sent from the Pope to Roman Catholic Churches throughout the world.) *Humanae Vitae* said that these birth control methods were not allowed. This made Paul unpopular among many Catholics, and effectively divided the Roman Catholic Church. The argument is still going on, as is Paul's decision that the ancient tradition forbidding priests to marry should stay.

The Anglican Communion

The Church of England is the *established* (official) church in England. The head of this Church is the English monarch, and the senior bishop is the *Archbishop of Canterbury*. Next to him in seniority is the Archbishop of York. The Church of England has a ruling council called a *Synod*, composed of bishops, priests and laity. The Synod votes on such decisions as whether to ordain women as priests. This means that the Archbishop of Canterbury is not in anything like the same position as the Pope in the Roman Catholic Church. He will have his say along with other bishops, but his vote counts equally with theirs. His authority is mainly in matters of administration, rather than belief.

There are now many churches all over the world which follow the teachings of the Church of England. However, because they do not recognise the Queen of England as their head, they cannot call themselves the Church of England. But to show that they follow the same teachings, they belong to what is called *the Anglican Communion*. Many of these Churches call themselves Episcopalian (meaning they have bishops), for example, the Episcopalian Church in Scotland (*not* the same as the Church of Scotland which is Presbyterian) and the Episcopalian Church in America. The Anglican Communion has members with widely differing beliefs. Some people call the Anglican church 'Protestant' but many Anglicans totally reject that title, referring to themselves as Catholics or 'Anglo-Catholics.'

The Protestant Churches

There are literally thousands of different denominations and groups which call themselves Protestant. Some of the best-known are the Baptists, United Reformed, and Lutheran. Most of the Protestant Churches trace their beliefs back to the Reformation, and to the teachings of Martin Luther and John Calvin especially. The Methodist Church, founded by followers of John Wesley, began as a breakaway movement from the Church of England; and the Salvation Army, founded by William Booth, broke away from the Methodist Church.

All Protestants regard the Bible as the basis of their faith and life. A few have bishops and priests, but most have ministers, or elders, and are run by councils.

One of the younger Churches in Britain today is the Pentecostal Church. The Pentecostal Church is popular among black communities, but not exclusively so.

In this picture you can see a Pentecostal choir singing at a joint evening service with a very different Christian group. There is a clue in the picture which should help you guess what the other Christian group is. Can you spot it?

Even in the more traditional and formal Churches, there is now plenty of room for self-expression, especially for the young. Here are five young men singing at a Roman Catholic Youth rally in Liverpool.

One of the newest and fastest-growing Christian movements today is the House Church Movement. *This is not an organised denomination; in fact, many of the members of House Churches joined their group specifically to get away from organised religion. In the days of the apostles, Christians met in one another's houses. Today, many Christians from all denominations have for a variety of personal reasons, left their church and joined a House group. Perhaps the most important thing about House Churches is that each one is self-governing. Each group has its own leaders (although some do not have leaders), and is self-financing. Some House Churches have Elders, but there is no ordained ministry of priests. There is no central organisation of House Churches, although there are national rallies for Christians who belong to these groups. Ironically, many House Churches have become so popular that they have had to buy Church buildings which are no longer in use in order to get all their members in!*

Christian communities

From the very early days of the Church's existence there have been some Christians who have found it difficult to practise their faith as they would wish while living in the world.

In the second and third centuries AD some men and women withdrew from society altogether, becoming hermits living in caves, or in the desert. Others withdrew from society but went to live in communities. We know these men and women as monks and nuns. The people living in these communities organise their lives on strict Christian principles, and also take vows which other Christians do not take. The three vows which have been most commonly taken are *poverty, chastity* and *obedience*. Some monastic communities are totally cut off from the world, their members living their lives totally within

These young men are considering their vocation *to the monastic life. They are talking to the Bishop of Lewes who is a monk as well as being a Bishop.*

the community. But others simply provide a base from which their members are sent out to work in the world. If you live in a big city, you may well have seen monks and nuns in the street, or at work perhaps in a school or hospital, or working as assistants to the priest in a parish. Monasticism has remained important in the Roman Catholic, Orthodox and Anglican traditions.

Twentieth-century communities

Taizé

Group activity

On the following pages you will find:
(a) A map of Taizé
(b) Information about your stay
(c) Tables of events for weekdays, Friday evenings, Saturday and Sunday
(d) A summary of a letter from Brother Roger to the United Nations.
What you have to do:
1   In your groups, make a list of everything you can discover about Taizé using *only* the information given.
2   Share your findings with those of the rest of the class.
3   Check your conclusions by reading more about Taizé. These are various books and visual aids available, as listed in the Resources at the end of the chapter.
4   Decide how you might arrange the information you have obtained, i.e. what headings might you use when writing notes about Taizé?
5   Write your own notes about Taizé.
6   Finally, look at the Appendix to this chapter for the background to the community.

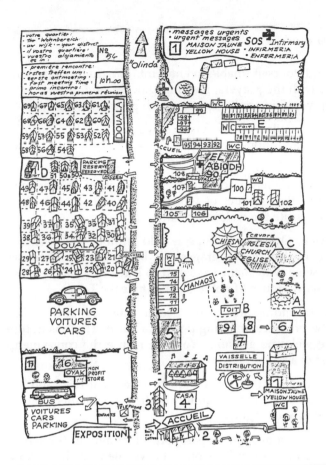

INFORMATION ABOUT YOUR STAY

As you arrive at Taizé, understand that it is part of the community's vocation to welcome you, so that you can reach the sources of God through prayer, through the silence of contemplation, through searching. To listen to you, if you want to speak about something which hurts you or which obstructs the paths of a search for the living God, some brothers remain in the church after the evening prayer: *perhaps being listened to in the church is a way for you to break through what blocks you or to discover a path for your life.*

You have come to Taizé to find a meaning to your life. One of Christ's secrets is that he loved you first. There lies the meaning of your life: to be loved for ever, to be clothed by God's forgiveness and trust, as if by a garment. In this way you will be able to take the risk of giving your life.

It is good, if you can, to finish your week at Taizé in silence, on Friday or Saturday. For many young people, a second week at Taizé, spent entirely in silence, proves to be a vital experience.

In the evening, silence, in the areas around the church, tents and huts, begins at the end of the evening prayer.

If you find yourself unable to enter into the rhythm and schedule of the day, with the prayers, meetings, meals, and times of silence, we will help you find another place which may better suit you.

The costs entailed by the visits of young people are not financed by any organisation. The meetings depend entirely on what you contribute.

The community never accepts any gifts for itself. It lives solely by its own work, the product of which is sold *only* at the 'Exposition', located opposite the welcome area.

At the café, Oyak, everything is sold without profit. It is the only place where alcoholic beverages may be consumed. Those who have brought wine with them are asked to leave it, until their departure, at the Yellow House (if not it is better to leave Taizé).

In the surrounding area, some people come trying to make a profit out of the presence of young people at Taizé. This has nothing to do with the welcome at Taizé. You can realise the consequences, and how best to act.

Both day and night, no one enters the villages of Taizé and Ameugny, in order to respect the tranquillity of their inhabitants. Some villagers request this of us regularly.

Do not leave your money, passport, or camera in the tents, chalets or houses; things can be stolen. Leave them at the Yellow House until departure.

The *Letter from Taizé* is a link between people, young and not so young, throughout the world. It is published in 9 languages. 8 pages every two months: giving news and accounts of the pilgrimage of trust on earth, suggesting themes for reflection in groups and parishes, containing texts for meditation and prayers and a bible reading for each day.

Sunday:
  8.45 am breakfast
10.00 am *Eucharist*
  2.30 pm meetings
  5.30 pm *common prayer*
  7.00 pm meal
  8.30 pm *evening prayer*

Friday evening: evening prayer followed by a prayer around the cross

Saturday evening: meeting with Brother Roger in the church after the evening prayer (simultaneous translation).

Weekdays
 8.00 am breakfast
 9.30 am *Eucharist* (with the life commitment of a brother of the
   community)
11.30 am meetings
 1.00 pm meal
 2.00 pm song practice
 3.30 pm meetings by countries of origin
 4.30 pm snack
 5.30 pm *common prayer*
 7.00 pm meal
 8.30 pm *evening prayer*

ON 2 JULY 1985, A GROUP OF CHILDREN WENT WITH BROTHER ROGER TO MEET THE SECRETARY GENERAL OF THE UNITED NATIONS.
THEY PUT SIX QUESTIONS TO HIM. Here is a summary of the introduction and the six questions.

Young people throughout the world are searching for a way to establish peace. It is for those who have no way of letting their voice be heard concerning the threat that hangs over their future that I, an old man, together with children, have come to the United Nations.

1   What changes can be suggested so that the UN may become a place where there is an eagerness to create trust between all peoples, and how can a council be set up which has the authority to stop wars from breaking out?
2   How can the UN persuade its members to stop prestige-spending and divert resources to more important needs, especially the needs of those who live in poverty; and will politicians refuse to accept any cult of their personality and all means of domination?
3   How can we ensure the fair distribution throughout the world of housing, health and food?
4   How can the UN take responsibility for the negotiations needed for general disarmament? The people of the world want peace. It is only a small handful in each country who have ambitions of expanding their power. They must be prevented from holding power.
5   What things are essential if the young are to be given the chance to contribute to the development of the whole world?
6   Many young people have the courage to be ambassadors of trust in places where there is mistrust. Will adults be ready to support these young people?

Iona

In the sixth century AD, St Columba used the Hebridean island of Iona as a base from which to carry the Christian message to the pagan lands of northern Britain. It was on this tiny island that he built a monastery, where it is believed the brothers produced the beautiful Book of Kells.

Today there are new Abbey buildings standing on Iona, the work of the Reverend George MacLeod. He was a Church of Scotland minister who worked in the shipyard areas of Glasgow during the great depression of the 1930s. He was struck by the feeling that the Church seemed to be totally irrelevant to the lives of the working class, and of unemployed people. In 1938 he moved to Iona with a group of ministers and unemployed craftsmen. Together they rebuilt Columba's ancient monastery. Initially MacLeod hoped that the people involved would learn what it is to live and work in a community, and that this knowledge would be taken back to be shared with others. Over the years, Iona has come to represent the Christian ideal for thousands of people.

The Iona Community now numbers 200 full members, and 800 associate members who come from all Christian denominations. The Community is especially dedicated to peace and the end of poverty. Unlike the Taizé community, members of the Iona Community do not take the traditional vows. This means that married men and women may become full members. The community rule instead insists on daily prayer and Bible study, giving 10 per cent of one's income to support the Church and the community, and working for peace and justice in one's own community. Also unlike traditional monastic communities, members of the Iona Community are not permanently resident on Iona. Apart from the two-year training period, every member returns to the island for one week each year for intensive seminars. Like Brother Roger at Taizé, MacLeod and the Community established by him are concerned with world problems like poverty, justice and peace. They believe that being a Christian is not simply a matter of developing one's spiritual or inner life. Being a Christian must influence the way you behave and the principles by which you live your life. Some Christians do not agree with this outlook, saying that the Church should not get involved with politics. Members of the community would argue that it is the duty of every Christian to speak out in the face of injustice. Not to speak out against evil is to give your assent to it happening.

The principles which lie behind the Iona Community's philosophy can be seen in its day-to-day activities. On the island, life is simple. Meat is only served twice a week, and never red meat. Eggs are free range, coffee is bought from a cooperative which ensures that the profits go to the growers, not to a Western manufacturer. No South African goods are bought. Members of the community are particularly active in Glasgow and Edinburgh, where they take part in social service projects. Also holidays for the young and for the disabled are offered on the island. Again as at Taizé, part of the work at Iona involves being a place where people can come to think, reflect and discuss with others the issues that concern them. About 2000 people a year visit Iona to take part in residential courses, and in addition there are 80 000 tourists and day-trippers who visit. Many of them make the journey because they have heard of the special atmosphere which this island conveys, and even people who do not consider themselves to be especially religious often talk of the sense of peace they have found on Iona.

Suggestions for coursework

1 Research: find out more about either Taizé or Iona and write a report. (K)

2 Explain why the following rules are observed at Iona (i.e. what they have to do with Christian principles):
    (a) only eating meat twice a week
    (b) never eating red meat
    (c) buying coffee from organisations which send the profits to the growers
    (d) never buying South African goods. (U)

3 Questions for evaluation: (E)
    (a) What do you think are the advantages and disadvantages of belonging to a community which is held together by common rules, but whose members live all over the world?
    (b) George MacLeod believed long ago that people living in the inner cities felt that the Church had nothing to offer them. Do you think he was right? Give reasons for your answer.

The Ecumenical Movement

One of the important things about Taizé and Iona is that they are both *ecumenical* communities – that is, they draw their members from all Christian denominations. The word 'ecumenical' comes from the Greek work *oikumene* which means 'the whole inhabited earth'. When Christians talk about the Ecumenical Movement they mean the movement among Christians to heal the divisions which exist among the Churches.

Jesus prayed that his followers should be one, in order that the whole world might be one. In fact, as we have seen, serious divisions have existed within the Church from the sixth century, and even more particularly since the sixteenth century. It was during the nineteenth century, when there was a revival of missionary activity, that Christian missionaries taking their message overseas suddenly realised how destructive these divisions were. It was acutely embarrassing to be preaching about this new religion which stressed love, peace and the oneness of the universe, when in the next village converts had been gained to another branch of the Church which refused to worship with your community. The first major move towards ecumenism was taken in 1910 at the International Missionary Conference in Edinburgh. This conference explored ways in which the Churches could collaborate and share resources in the mission field. After this conference the 'Faith and Order' movement began. This was a group of Christians who looked specifically at the differences among the Churches on matters of belief and authority. In 1927 an international conference was held at Lausanne to look at these very questions. Some representatives of the Orthodox Church took part, but the Roman Catholic Church sent no representatives. Through this conference, and at another, ten years later at Edinburgh, members of different Churches came to understand more about each other, the differences which divided them and the common ground between them.

The World Council of Churches

In 1948 the World Council of Churches came into existence. The 146 founder-member Churches could all agree that the belief they held in common was in Jesus Christ as God and Saviour. The WCC is an international fellowship of Churches seeking ways in which they can act together. The number of Churches belonging to the WCC is growing all the time. Perhaps the most important event was the arrival of the Russian Orthodox Church and the first of the Pentecostal churches in 1961. Also in that year the Roman Catholic Church sent official observers, having had nothing to do with the WCC previously. By 1980 there were 293 member Churches, many of which came from developing countries. This means that the WCC is becoming increasingly international, and is losing its originally 'white English-speaking' image.

There are five important units in the WCC.

(i) The Faith and Order Commission, which looks at issues on which the Churches are divided.

(ii) World Mission and Evangelism, which looks at ways in which the Churches can work together in proclaiming the Gospel.

(iii) Church and Society, which looks at the relationship between the Christian faith and today's world, especially science and technology.

(iv) Dialogue with People of Living Faiths, which seeks understanding between Christians and members of the other great world faiths.

(v) Theological Education, which helps the Church prepare people for mission and ministry.

The British Council of Churches

The foundation of the WCC inspired the creation of the British Council of Churches. It has five important departments:

Christian Aid
Community Affairs
Ecumenical Affairs
International Affairs
Conference for World Mission

Moves towards unity

However, in spite of all this activity, there remain several thousand separate Churches in the world. Many Christians would say that this in itself is no bad thing. What is harmful is the fact that some of these Churches refuse to recognise members of other Churches as 'true Christians', or that some Churches refuse to share the Eucharist (Holy Communion) with other Churches. There have been two particular moves towards actually uniting different Churches, as illustrated in the two photos following.

Every year, in January, there is a Week of Prayer for Christian Unity, when Christians of most denominations meet together for prayer, and decide on ways in which they can work together.

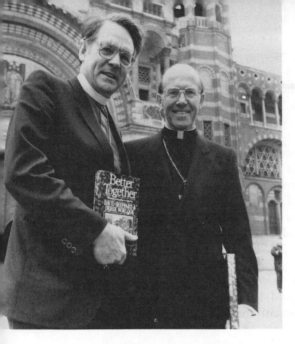

The Roman Catholic Archbishop of Liverpool, Derek Warlock, and the Anglican bishop David Sheppard have for many years been setting an example of the way in which Churches can work together for the good of their community. Now they have written a book called Better Together.

The Church of South India

In 1947 the South India United Church, the Methodist Church of South India and the Anglican church of South India joined together as the Church of South India. One of the biggest problems (the union took 30 years to negotiate!) was the matter of leadership. The Anglican Church had bishops and ordained clergy, the other Churches did not. Ever since the Reformation this has remained one of the thorniest issues between the Churches. Eventually the Church of South India accepted the idea of having bishops and priests, but so as not to create a barrier between priests and lay people, instituted a form of government by elected synod.

The United Reformed Church

In 1972 the Congregational Church (England and Wales) and Presbyterian Church (England) united to form the URC.

There have been other attempts at forming union between Churches, such as the lengthy discussions between the Church of England and the Methodist Church in the 1970s. So far, however, no other union has taken place, although Churches continue to grow in their understanding of each other.

Most of the discussions which have taken place have been between Church leaders. Over recent years there is evidence of more 'grass-roots' Christians working together and worshipping together. Many Christians, while continuing to worship at their traditional church on Sundays, are taking part in ecumenical prayer meetings in each other's houses during the week. There are many examples of monthly ecumenical services – often non-Eucharistic. To some people the divisions seem nonsense. But there are issues which matter very much to Christians of different denominations. These issues cause problems which are very difficult to solve.

1   Authority. Should there be special people ordained to have authority to teach and administer the sacraments? Or should all Christians be allowed to do these things?

2   Should women be ordained?

3   Attitudes to the Bible – the most conservative view states that the Bible contains *all* truth necessary for salvation. Others claim that the traditions of the Church are also important. (See pp.22–4.)

Suggestions for coursework

1   Find out about any activities in your area which are run by Churches of different denominations working together. Write a report.   (K)

2   What are the major differences which divide Christians?   (U)

3   Find out as much as you can about the work of *either* the World Council of Churches *or* the British Council of Churches.   (K)

4   What in your opinion have been the major achievements of the WCC/BCC?   (E)

5   In what ways do you consider the divisions between the churches to be (a) harmful, (b) an advantage?   (E)

Modern evangelism

In 1984 Billy Graham made a return visit to Britain. Mission England, who organised the tour, had to hire football stadiums in order to pack everyone in. Crowds of 20000–30000 were not unusual, and people were prepared to travel 150 miles to hear probably the best-known modern evangelist. Like many other American evangelists Billy Graham has learnt to make full use of the media. During his three-month mission he appeared on TV, was interviewed by all the press and met the leaders of all the main Churches in the country.

I am going to ask you to get up out of your seats, and come forward, and stand in front of this platform to say symbolically, 'I want to open my heart to Christ'.

Over the three-month period, over a million people went to hear Dr Graham's rallies. The climax of every rally was when Billy Graham issued his famous invitation (see picture and caption on page 21).

In all, 97 000 people came forward.

In the same year Billy Graham went to Russia, where he was the guest of the Russian Orthodox Church. While he was there he met political leaders and discussed with them issues like human rights and the nuclear threat. He was invited to return.

Questions for discussion

1   Why do you think Billy Graham and others like him regard mission as so important? (See Matthew 28:16–20; Acts 1:6–11.)
2   Do *all* Christians have a duty to preach their faith to others?

Research

Find out about:
   (a) TV evangelism in the USA.
   (b) drive-in churches in the USA.
Do you think either of these could become popular in Britain? (About 6 million people watch *Songs of Praise* every week.)

The Bible

The Bible is a very special book for all Christians.

The Bible is used in worship by most Christian denominations, and many people read it privately on most days. Some Christians believe that the Bible is factually true because it was revealed directly by God to the people who wrote it. Others believe that although the books of the Bible contain great wisdom, they do not contain historical truth. Some believe that only the Church leaders have the authority to interpret the Bible (i.e. say what it means), while others believe that every Christian must use his/her own intelligence in understanding it. (See pp. 145–50.) Nevertheless, although Christians hold very different views about the Bible, the book still binds all Christians together.

The Bible as we now have it took hundreds of years to be written and compiled. It is not one book, but a collection of many books, written by many different authors. The Old Testament is the collection of holy books of the Jews which was read by the very first followers of Jesus (who were all Jewish). It was not until three hundred years after Jesus that the Church decided which books should be included in the New Testament. In some Bibles there is also a section between the Old and New Testaments called the Apocrypha. This section contains 'disputed' books which are not regarded as genuine by Jews, and which do not appear in many Protestant Bibles.

Group activity

Here are two excerpts from early Christian writings. They are both concerned with the problem of knowing what books were to be accepted in the New Testament (which one of them calls the canon) and which were not. Read the passages carefully.

We receive the Revelation of John. We also accept the Apocalypse of Peter, although some of *our friends will not have it read in Church*. But 'The Shepherd' was written *quite recently in our own times*, in the city of Rome, and although it should be read, *it cannot be publicly read in Church* to the people.

(Adapted from the Muratorian Fragment c. AD 190)

One letter of Peter – the first – is accepted. But the tradition we received says that the second is not in the canon. But as for the Acts of Peter, the Gospel of Peter and the Apocalypse of Peter, we know that *they were not handed down among the writings*, for *no Church writer either in ancient times or in our own day has quoted from them*.

We ought also to be aware that some people have rejected the letter to the Hebrews, because they say that the church in Rome says that *Paul did not write it*.

And since *Paul mentions in the letter to the Romans one Hermas*, who is said to be the author of 'The Shepherd', many people judge it to be an essential book, although others dispute it. As we know, *it has actually come to be read publicly in Churches* and *some of the oldest writers have quoted from it*.

The Revelation of John is rejected by some, but others give it a place among the acknowledged writings.

(Adapted from Eusebius, *History of the Church*, c. AD 330)

Something to discuss and write about

1   Make a list of books mentioned by either or both of these writers which were 'disputed' (that is, some people did not accept them as Scripture).
2   Which (if any) of these disputed books are in the New Testament now (i.e. they were accepted in the end)?
3   According to the Muratorian Fragment, what is the sign that a book *is* accepted?
4   According to Eusebius:
    (a) How can it be proved that the books said to be written by Peter should not be accepted?
    (b) Why did the Roman Church refuse to accept the letter to the Hebrews?
    (c) Why did some people want to include 'The Shepherd' of Hermas among the accepted books?
    (d) What two pieces of evidence show Eusebius that some people *have* accepted 'The Shepherd'?
5   Write a summary to explain what we learn from these two writings about how books came to be included in the New Testament.

Clue! A book has three characteristics – think about who wrote it, how it was used, where it was read. What do these facts tell us about the *authority* of the book?

Summary

During the first three centuries after the lifetime of Jesus, many Christian books were being written, and many Christians were writing lists (like the ones you have read) of the books which they considered to be *canonical* – that is, accepted as Scripture. Books which were accepted would be regarded as having the same authority as the Old Testament – they would be looked upon as the word of God. The four Gospels, Matthew, Mark, Luke and John, were never disputed; neither were most of Paul's letters. To be accepted as Scripture a book had to be written by one of the apostles, or by someone known to an apostle, such as Luke. It had to have been read aloud in Church meetings from the earliest days, and must be a book that could be quoted from as an authority by other Christians.

The Bible is now translated into hundreds of languages. There are many English translations. Which one do you use at school, and why?

Creeds

There are two very ancient statements of belief called *Creeds*. The word 'creed' comes from the Latin word *credo* which means 'I believe' Christians from most of the larger denominations say the creeds during their acts of worship. The Creeds are the most important Christian beliefs, and as with the Bible, individual Christians will interpret the statements differently.

The Apostles' Creed

I believe in God, the Father almighty,
creator of heaven and earth.

I believe in Jesus Christ, his only Son, our Lord.
He was conceived by the power of the Holy Spirit
and born of the Virgin Mary.
He suffered under Pontius Pilate,
was crucified, died, and was buried.
He descended to the dead.
On the third day he rose again.
He ascended into heaven,
and is seated at the right hand of the Father.
He will come again to judge the living and the dead.

I believe in the Holy Spirit,
the holy catholic Church,
the communion of saints,
the forgiveness of sins,
the resurrection of the body,
and the life everlasting. Amen.

The Nicene Creed
We believe in one God,
the Father, the almighty,
maker of heaven and earth,
of all that is,
seen and unseen.

We believe in one Lord, Jesus Christ,
the only Son of God,
eternally begotten of the Father,
God from God, Light from Light,
true God from true God,
begotten, not made,
of one Being with the Father.
Through him all things were made.
For us men and for our salvation
he came down from heaven;
by the power of the Holy Spirit
he became incarnate of the Virgin Mary, and was made man.
For our sake he was crucified under Pontius Pilate;
he suffered death and was buried.
On the third day he rose again
in accordance with the Scriptures;
he ascended into heaven
and is seated at the right hand of the Father.
He will come again in glory
to judge the living and the dead,
and his kingdom will have no end.

We believe in the Holy Spirit,
the Lord, the giver of life,
who proceeds from the Father and the Son.
With the Father and the Son he is worshipped and glorified.
He has spoken through the Prophets.

We believe in one holy catholic and apostolic Church.
We acknowledge one baptism for the forgiveness of sins.
We look for the resurrection of the dead,
and the life of the world to come.   Amen.

Both Creeds state that Christians believe in the 'Holy *catholic* Church'.
The word *catholic* means 'universal' or 'worldwide'. It is important to
Christians that, by keeping the traditional creeds, they are acknow-
ledging that for all their differences, they still belong to a single
worldwide family.

The Trinity
Christians of all denominations are bound together by their belief in
the *Trinity*. This is a doctrine which expresses Christian belief in God,
and you will find it referred to all through this book, but often in its
better-known form of *God the Father, Son and Holy Spirit*. Christianity
teaches that although there is only one God, yet that one God is at

the same time Father, Son and Holy Spirit. For the last two thousand years Christian teachers have been trying to explain exactly how God can be 'Three in One'. Perhaps some of the easiest explanations to follow are those using symbols.

St Patrick is said to have used the *shamrock* as a symbol for the Trinity, because, like the clover, it is only one leaf, and yet it is made up of three leaves.

Other teachers have used the sun as a symbol. We only see the sun, yet we know that light and heat also come from the sun – so, in a way, light, heat and the ball of gas we call the sun are all one.

Another useful comparison – although not an exact one – is that of light. We think of light as being 'white', but if you look at a rainbow, or through a prism, we know that in fact 'white' light is made up of several colours.

Something to think about
See if you can think of any good symbols for the Trinity.

Most Christians do not spend hours trying to explain the doctrine of the Trinity. They accept it as a mystery. One writer put it like this:

> Frank lit his pipe and said, 'You know, there are four things I like about the Trinity. First, I love having a father in God. Second, I love having a friend and brother in Jesus. Third, I love having a comforter and guide in the Holy Spirit. And fourth . . .'
>
> Anne and I said, 'Yes?'
>
> 'Fourth, I love the fact that it's a mystery. God in three persons. Three-persons - one God. It's a mystery and I love it. Why would I want to spoil things by trying to explain it?'
>
> Adrian Plass, *The Horizontal Epistles of Andromeda Veal* (Marshall Pickering, 1988)

Appendix
In 1940, a young man called Roger Shutz bought a house at Taizé in France, with the intention of establishing a community with a group of like-minded young men. Living during the war, Shutz was struck more than anything else by the tragedy of hatred and disunity between people of different nationalities, and even Christians belonging to different Churches. 'Brother Roger', as Shutz became, has spent his life working for *reconciliation* – healing the divisions which exist between people. Like traditional monastic orders, the monks at Taizé take the vows of poverty, chastity and obedience, but they also stress the need for joy, simplicity, mercy and hope in their lives, and for the future of the world. Today there are members of the community from all Christian traditions – Roman Catholic, Orthodox and Protestant – and from about 20 different countries. Most of the monks live at Taizé, but sometimes groups of them go to work in

areas of the world where they are needed, especially areas experiencing poverty and deprivation.

'Going to Taizé' became popular among young people in the 1960s and has remained so ever since. One of the chief functions for the community is to be a place where people searching for meaning and truth in their lives can spend time together in quietness, discussion, meditation and prayer. Young people from all over the world spend a week at Taizé, and when they return home are encouraged to meet together at intervals to continue to reflect on the insights gained on their visit.

Resources
NB Many of these resources will be of use throughout the course of study.

Books
D. B. Barrett, *World Christian Encyclopedia* (Oxford University Press)
J. R. Bailey, *Founders, Prophets and Sacred Books* (Schofield & Sims)
A. Brown, *The Christian World* (Macdonald)
A. Brown, *The Lion History of Christianity* (Lion)
K. Ottosson, *The Pentecostal Churches* (REP)
M. Ward, *The Protestant Christian Churches* (Ward Lock)
S. Hackel, *The Orthodox Church* (Ward Lock)
P. Kelly, *Roman Catholicism* (Ward Lock)
D. Naylor, *Jesus: an Enquiry* (Macmillan Education)
R. Duckworth, *The Gospel in the Making* (Macmillan Education)
J. Allen, *The Way of the Christians* (Hulton)
J. Thompson, *Christian Belief and Practice* (Arnold)
T. Shannon, *Jesus* (Chichester Project) (Lutterworth)
P. Curtis, *Exploring the Bible* (Chichester Project) (Lutterworth)
P. Curtis, *The Christians' Book* (Chichester Project) (Lutterworth)
I. Wilson, *Jesus, the Evidence* (Weidenfeld)
L. Brockett, *The Ecumenical Movement* (CEM)
B. Lealman, *The Face of Christ* (CEM)
B. Lealman, *Churches in Britain Today* (CEM)
G. Read, J. Rudge, R. Howarth, *The Westhill Project* (Mary Glasgow)

Audio-visual aids
Christianity in India (Bury Peerless)
Believe it or not series (ITV)
Jesus of Nazareth (Precision Video)
Christianity through the eyes of Christian Children (CEM Video)

Answer to Question 3 on p.5: *Spanish*

2 Sacraments and ceremonies of commitment

Objectives for Chapter 2

1 What you should KNOW.
The major sacraments and rituals practised within Christianity: baptism (various forms); Confirmation; The Holy Matrimony; funerals; penance; anointing the sick; Ordination.

2 What you should UNDERSTAND.
(a) *New words and technical terms*
Commitment; Holy Spirit; repent; sin; charismatic; sacrament; ordination; anointing; confession; penance.
(b) *People, writings and traditions*
(i) People: the importance of priests, ministers and lay people.
(ii) the authority of the Bible as the foundation of Christian practice.
(iii) Tradition: the various traditions within the Church regarding the way in which rituals are conducted, e.g. infant or believer's baptism, varying beliefs about divorce.
(c) *Belief*
Rebirth; cleansing; dedication; repentance; symbolism; the importance of sacraments; original sin.
(d) *Moral issues*
Should children be initiated into a religious faith before they can decide for themselves?
Should everyone have a right to be married in church?
Should people who have been divorced be allowed a second church wedding?
(e) *Questions about the meaning of life*
Is baptism necessary for salvation? Is there life after death? Why do people keep traditions? Are rites of passage important?

3 What you should be able to DO.
Evaluate on the basis of evidence and argument questions arising out of the study of this chapter.

Something to discuss and write about
What is commitment? The following is to help you find out.

Ian Rush played a magnificent match this afternoon. The lad always shows great *commitment* to the game.   (*Grandstand*, BBC)

Susan has worked hard this term, showing determination and *commitment* to her work.   (School report)

1   *Word associations* In pairs, play a game of word associations. One of you says 'commitment' and the other says the first word he or she thinks of. Write down all the words you think of, and then compare your words with those of the rest of the class. Now see if the class can agree on a definition of the word 'commitment'. Write the meaning down.
2   The sports commentator said that Rush showed *commitment* to the game. What qualities in Rush's game do you think made the commentator say this? How might Rush have *shown* his commitment?
3   Susan's school report said that she had shown *commitment* to her work. How do you think she might have shown this commitment?
4   (a) Discuss with your partner what it means to be *committed* to a cause or a project.
     (b) What sort of things will you *not* do if you are so committed?
     (c) Try to think of one or two causes, projects or beliefs which people become committed to. How might this *commitment* affect their lives?
5   Discuss with your partner any causes, etc., which *you* feel committed to. Does this commitment make any difference to the way you behave, or the things you might do?

Signs of commitment
Most people do feel commitment to at least one thing in life. It may be a club, a sport, a hobby, their job, or their family. Sometimes people who want to show their commitment to a group or organisation go through a special ceremony when they join. Sometimes they may wear special clothes which tell everyone that they belong to the group.

What might members or supporters of the following organisations do to show their commitment to that group?
(a) The Girl Guides
(b) Save the Children Fund
(c) The Campaign Against Blood Sports
(d) Campaign for Nuclear Disarmament

Christian commitment

The idea of commitment is very important in Christianity. At various stages in their lives, many Christians (although not all) go through ceremonies, and make promises which show their commitment to Jesus in a special way.

Look at these photographs:

A

B
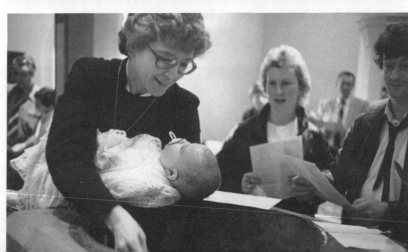

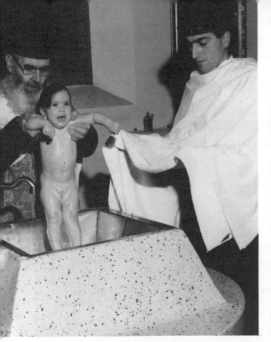

C

D

Test your knowledge (in pairs or groups)

1 What is taking place in these photographs?
2 Try to name the *denomination* of Christians in each photograph. Give reasons for your choice in each case.
3. Look at picture A. What is different about this picture compared to all the others?
4 Look at picture B.
(a) What is the title of the woman holding the baby?
(b) She has her hand in a bowl. What is the correct name for this 'bowl'? Where in a Church would it usually be found, and why?
5 Look at picture C. Find *two* things in this picture which are different from pictures A and B.
6 Look at picture D. What is different in this picture compared to all the others?
7 What do pictures A, C and D have in common?
  You will have discovered by now that these four photographs show the ceremony of *baptism* in different Churches.

Finding out how Christian baptism began

Each group will need: a New Testament, and someone who is good at anagrams! If you do not know the answer, try to work it out from clue 1. If you still can't do it, use clue 2.

Task A

1 Who is the first person mentioned in the New Testament who baptised people?
  Clue 1 BNTPHJEATTSOHI (*3 words*)
  Clue 2 Mark 1:4

2   What did people have to do in order to be baptised?
    Clue 1 PTEENR
    Clue 2 Matthew 3:2
3   Complete this sentence.
    Baptism was a sign that a person's . . . had been. . . .
    Clue: Luke 3:3
4   (a) Where did John baptise people?
        Clue 1 VONDRJRREAI (*2 words*)
        Clue 2 Mark 1:5.
(b) Which of the pictures on pp. 30 and 31 do you think looks most
like the sort of baptism that John carried out? Do you think the similarity
is an accident, or do you think it is deliberate? Give reasons for your
answer.
5   Complete this sentence.
    John baptised people with water. He said that one coming after him,
who would be 'mightier than' himself would baptise with the . . . (*2
words*)
    Clue 1. Mark 1:8 / Luke 3:16
    Who do you think John meant when he said, 'one mightier than I'?
6   Write one or two sentences explaining why people came to John to
be baptised.

Task B

Read Mark 16:15–16a and Matthew 28:19.
    Explain in your own words why you think that most Christians practise
baptism. (You should try to use some of these words: Jesus; command;
Bible; authority.)
    You will have discovered that according to the New Testament, John
the Baptist baptised Jesus, and that Jesus told his disciples to travel
all over the world telling people about himself. If the people who listened
to them *repented*, their *sins* would be forgiven, and they would receive
the *Holy Spirit*. Most Churches today follow Jesus's command and
baptise new members.

STOP

Before you go on, make sure that you understand these words:
    baptism/baptise; sin; repent/repentance;
    forgive/forgiveness/forgiven.
    denomination; Holy Spirit.
If you are not sure about the meaning of a word, try to write a
sentence using the word correctly. Show the sentence to your teacher
to check that you were right.

Exploring the meaning of baptism

If we only had the New Testament evidence about baptism, many
questions would not be answered.
    Here are two of the questions people ask. How would you answer
them?

(a) Does anything actually happen at baptism? Is it *just* a sign that a person is making a commitment to their faith, or does God actually *do* something which in some way changes the person being baptised?
(b) If baptism is a sign that a person's sins have been forgiven, isn't it nonsense to baptise babies who can't have sinned?

In pairs, write down any other questions about baptism which you would like answered at this stage. Present your questions to the class and see if anyone has any suggestions as to how they might be answered.

It is likely that in the early days of the Church's existence, people asked questions rather like the ones you have asked. Church leaders like St Paul, or later, bishops and presbyters, and people called the 'Fathers' of the Church had to answer these questions. The answers they gave were remembered and later written down. These answers have become the *Tradition* of the Church. Over the last 2000 years there have been divisions in the Church, and each of the separate Churches (denominations) developed its own *traditions* which may be different from any of the others. You have discovered some of these differences by looking at the photographs.

> ### Something to discuss
> You will have noticed from the beginning of this chapter that water is essential for baptism. Water is a very important symbol in Christianity. Apart from drinking it, what do you do with water every day?
>   So – what do you think is the point of being baptised in water? Why do you think that some Christians still insist on being baptised in *running* water?

A deeper meaning
It is easy to see that being baptised in water is a symbolic action showing that your sins have been 'washed away', and the use of running water emphasises this symbolism. But the use of water has a deeper meaning which is not easy to grasp.
Water gives life. . . . Water is one of the few things which is absolutely necessary if we are to live. Without water, we die.
Water kills. . . . If you stay under water for too long, you drown.
  Now look at the following pieces of information.
1   Look back at pictures A, C and D on pp.30–31. You can see that in the Orthodox, Baptist and Pentecostal Churches, the person being baptised is actually plunged *into* the water.
2   St Paul writing to the Romans (6:4)

> By our baptism then, we were *buried* with him (Jesus) and shared in his *death*, in order that, just as Christ was *raised from death* by the glorious power of the Father, so also we might *live* a new life.

3 Heavenly father, by the power of your Holy Spirit you give to your faithful people *new life* in the *waters of Baptism.*

Baptism is the sign that . . . we are united with him in his *death* . . . we are *raised* with Christ to new *life* in the Spirit.

We thank you that through the deep *waters of death* you brought your Son, and *raised* him to life in triumph.

(from the Church of England Baptism Service)

Paul's letter, the Church of England service and the Orthodox and Baptist baptism rites all tell us something about the deeper meaning of water in baptism.

It is to do with (a) what is happening to the person going into the water, and (b) life and death.

Working in pairs or in groups, try to write an explanation of the meaning of water in Baptism. Compare your definition with those of other groups.

You should now be able to work out why Baptism used to be, and in some Churches still is, carried out especially at Easter time.

Light in Baptism
Light is another important symbol in Christianity, often used in Baptism. In the Orthodox, Roman Catholic and Anglican traditions, the baby (or adult) being baptised is given a candle which is sometimes lit from the Paschal (Easter) candle. Many children light their candle on the anniversary of their baptism.

In the Anglican ceremony, the person baptising hands the candle to the person baptised (or the godparents in the case of a baby), with the words:

Receive this light,
This is to show that you have passed from darkness to light.
Shine as a light in the world to the glory of God the Father.

What do you think is the meaning of the words in italics?

The vows
At Baptism it is usual for the Baptised to make a statement of faith. This will often mean answering simple questions. If the baptised are babies, then adults answer for them. When a baby is baptised these will be the godparents.
In the Anglican service the godparents are asked:

Do you turn to Christ?
Do you repent of your sins?
Do you renounce evil?

The Priest or Minister then signs the baby on the forehead with the sign of the cross.

Later the godparents have to declare that they 'believe and trust' in God the Father, his Son Jesus Christ, and in the Holy Spirit.

The Spirit and Baptism

The story of a baptism long ago
Some years after Jesus died, Simon Peter, one of his closest followers, baptised a Roman soldier named Cornelius. You can read the story in Acts, Chapter 10, of how not only Cornelius but his whole household (which would have included children and slaves) became Christians. There is an interesting detail in this story. Virtually all Christians at this time were Jewish by birth, and many of them did not believe that it was the will of God that a non-Jew should become a Christian. But as a sign that Cornelius and his household *should* be baptised, they were given the gift of the Holy Spirit. Other Christians knew that they had received the Spirit because they could be heard *'speaking in tongues of ecstasy'*. Some Christians today believe in the 'baptism of the Spirit', which happens when they too are given the gift of 'speaking in tongues'. It is very difficult for anyone who has not experienced 'speaking in tongues', or 'glossolalia', to understand what it is like. People who have experienced it say that it is like being taken over by the power of the Spirit. They praise God in a language unknown to other people, although some people who do not have the 'gift of tongues' do have the gift of 'interpreting tongues'.

Charismatic worship *These people have the gift of tongues – a gift of the Spirit. This sort of worship used to be associated only with Pentecostal and Free Churches, but now it is also becoming more common in Anglican and Roman Catholic Churches.*

Not all Christians believe that this is a gift of the Spirit and in fact some disapprove of 'speaking in tongues'. For them the 'Spirit' can only be given through the sacraments.

Baptism as a sacrament

Most Churches teach that baptism is a *sacrament*. A *sacrament* is a visible sign that God's power is present. Most Protestant Churches including some Anglicans say that there are only two sacraments – Baptism and Holy Communion, but the Orthodox, Roman Catholic and some Anglican Churches teach that there are seven sacraments. (We shall be finding out about the others later in this chapter.) Christians believe that God gives *grace* through sacraments. *Grace* is special power to help you do the will of God. You may often hear Christian prayers which use the words, 'Give us grace to. . .'. This means, 'Give us the power and strength' to do whatever it is.

We have looked at baptism as a time when a person makes a commitment to follow a new way of life (or makes that commitment on behalf of a child). But it is also seen as a time when God makes a commitment to give the new Christian the strength to follow the Christian life with all its demands. Orthodox Christians emphasise this aspect of Baptism. They say that baptism should not be seen as a sign that a person has made a conscious decision to become a Christian. It is a sacrament where God gives the child grace to live a Christian life.

The Roman Catholic Church also stresses that baptism is a sacrament at which grace is given. The baby is annointed with oil (chrism), and the priest touches its ears and mouth, saying, 'The Lord Jesus made the deaf hear and the dumb speak. May he touch your ears to receive his word and your mouth to proclaim his faith'.

Original sin

There are people who, for various reasons, behave in an anti-social way because they are not able to control themselves. For example, we call some people kleptomaniacs if they cannot stop stealing. Because they cannot help themselves, they are usually sent to a doctor or psychiatrist who helps them overcome the problem. Christians who believe that God's grace is given at the sacrament of baptism see the whole human race rather as a psychiatrist sees a kleptomaniac – they are people who do wrong because they cannot help it – at least, not without outside assistance.

We saw earlier that some people say that there is no point in baptising babies (a) because they are too young to decide for themselves whether they believe, and (b) because baptism is a sign of repentance and babies have not sinned. It is true that a baby cannot do 'wrong' because it does not know what 'wrong' is. But some Christians believe in *original sin*. It is said that human beings were made 'in the image of God' and that, like God, they could not sin. But at some stage (some people say it was Adam and Eve who were responsible) humans disobeyed God – in fact they tried to override him and refused to accept his authority over them. The guilt of this first (or original) sin was passed on, almost like an hereditary illness, to the whole human race. That is why, it is said, humans have a tendency to sin and do wrong, and that is why they need the *grace* of God if they are to overcome this tendency.

STOP

Before you go on, make sure that you can explain the meaning of the following in connection with baptism:

water, original sin; waters of death; new life; Holy Spirit; sacrament; light; grace.

Revision

Understanding the symbolism of baptism – and Orthodox baptism
The Orthodox ceremony is very ancient indeed, and full of symbolic actions and effects. You should by now understand the beliefs associated with baptism well enough to do the following exercise. Here are 6 photographs in sequence showing the stages in an Orthodox baptism. For each photograph, write a brief explanation of what is taking place and explain *why* you think it is being done. You could imagine that these pictures are slides and that you have been asked to write a commentary on them for a lesson with a third-year class at your school. (Answers on p. 60 at the end of the chapter.)

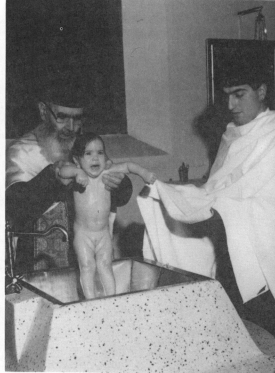

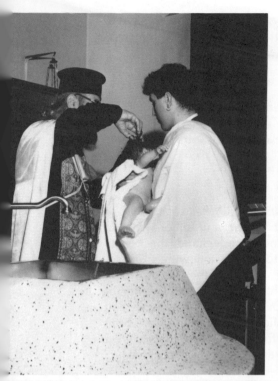

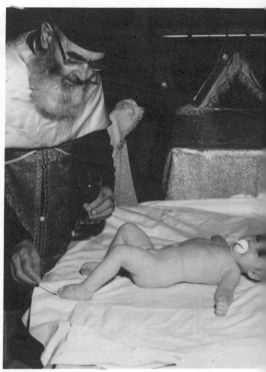

Benjamin's baptism – Dave's story

It is not unusual for babies to be born at times when most people would rather be asleep. Benjamin was born at 4.15 a.m., after Jane had been in hospital for eight hours. It was when he failed to breathe that all the plans we had made for his arrival became irrelevant. No one panicked. But within minutes, Benjamin's life was depending on plastic tubes, electronic gear, oxygen supplies and the skill of doctors and nurses. During a lull in the tests and examinations that followed, a polaroid photograph of Benjamin was taken for us. All part of the concern for the parents as well as the baby, but it said loud and clear, 'This may be all you have'.

Then we were asked, 'Would you like him to be baptised?'

We didn't need to discuss it. We both said no. Even before that question was asked, we knew that Benjamin might easily die. But whatever his condition he did not *need* baptism to be sure of God's love. We felt he was already God's child as well as ours.

In a way we had already discussed the issue when talking to our friend Cathy about her fear that her baby was in some way damned or destined for limbo if she were not baptised. We did not believe that baptism was some sort of magic, but that it was a commitment to bring up the child in the knowledge of Christ and of Christian ways of thinking. It is also an opportunity for people in Christ's Church to welcome the child into the family of all Christian people.

In the Church of England, to which we both belong, it is customary to baptise babies, although there is no law about this. Jane was herself baptised in the Church of England when she was one year old. In contrast, I was not baptised until I was 15 years old. The Baptist Church, of which my parents were members, regarded baptism as something which adults decided for themselves.

Before Benjamin was born, Jane and I had decided on two of the godparents. We felt that the role of godparents was to share in the Christian upbringing of the child. Having godparents extends the child's family in a special way. We had decided on two godparents before Benjamin was born, and while he was in hospital we asked two further friends to be godparents, making four in all – two men and two women. Benjamin was to be baptised within the Church of England, at our local Church which we regularly attended. It happened that two of the godparents were members of the Church of England, but the other two were Roman Catholic. Our only concern was that they believed in the commitment they were to make.

When he was three months old, Benjamin was baptised, kicking and screaming, as part of the regular Sunday morning Eucharist. We could have had a private ceremony in the afternoon, as some people do, but if Benjamin was to be welcomed into the Church through his baptism, it made sense for the members of this little branch of the Church to be there. We and the godparents made our promises on his behalf. The occasion was heavily overladen with emotions of thankfulness and relief that he was alive. He had very nearly died, but now we had come to his baptism, not as an emergency measure in case he died, but looking forward, seeing that ceremony as an important stage in his upbringing within the Christian family.

Elizabeth's baptism

Elizabeth's father Robert is a vicar. When she was born, Robert and his wife Helen discussed when Elizabeth should be baptised. Helen wanted Elizabeth to be baptised as soon as possible, but Robert said, 'I would much rather wait until she is old enough to be aware of what is happening. I agree with infant baptism, but some of the nicest baptisms I've ever done have been with children aged two or three. They can talk, and can understand some of what their parents say to them. They know that it is a special day, rather like a birthday, and they remember it. It seems a pity that we baptise babies at an age when they have no chance of remembering the event.'

But Helen was still unhappy, and in the end Robert agreed to baptise Elizabeth at six weeks, for Helen's peace of mind. 'I can't really explain it', said Helen. 'I just know that if she died and hadn't been baptised I'd be really worried. Perhaps it is just superstition, but it's how I feel. I somehow didn't feel that she was a *whole* person until after her baptism.'

Something to discuss and write about

1   Helen and Cathy were both anxious that their babies should be baptised. Try to explain in your own words *why* they were anxious. What did Cathy mean by the words 'damned' and 'limbo'?

2   Explain why Dave and Jane did not have Benjamin baptised when he was dangerously ill. What do you think Cathy would have done in the same situation?

3   In your own words explain Dave's understanding of baptism. How is his understanding different from that of the Orthodox and Roman Catholic traditions? Do you think that Dave's understanding was influenced by his Baptist upbringing?

4   When Benjamin was in hospital there was a baby in the next bed called Sophie. She had serious brain damage, never became conscious, and after a week she died. Just before she died, her parents asked the hospital Chaplain to baptise her, even though they were not regular churchgoers. Why do you think they wanted her baptised?

5   Explain the importance of godparents as Dave sees it. Do you agree with his attitude? Do you think it matters that two of Benjamin's godparents were Roman Catholic even though he was baptised in the Church of England? Do you think some Roman Catholics would object?

6   Why did Dave and Jane want Benjamin baptised during the Eucharist rather than at a private ceremony?

7   If you had a baby who was in danger of dying, and someone said 'Do you want the baby to be baptised?', what do you think your decision would be, and why?

Confirmation

In the Roman Catholic, Anglican and Methodist Churches in particular, there is a ceremony called *Confirmation*. At this ceremony, people who were baptised as babies and who have now decided for themselves that they want to lead a Christian life, make their own commitment, and take responsibility for the promises that their godparents made for them at their baptism.

STOP

Check your understanding
Why is there no ceremony of adult Confirmation in
(a) the Baptist Church?
(b) the Orthodox Church?

In Roman Catholic and Anglican Churches, confirmation is carried out by the *bishop*. At the Roman Catholic service the candidate is anointed with holy oil (chrism), and the Bishop says, 'Receive the seal of the gift of the Holy Spirit'.
The candidates are asked to declare their faith:
Do you turn to Christ?
Do you repent of your sins?
Do you renounce evil?
They are asked about their belief:
Do you believe and trust in God the father who made the world?
Do you believe and trust in his son Jesus Christ who redeemed mankind?
Do you believe and trust in his Holy Spirit who gives life to the people of God?

These Italian children in London going for Confirmation are dressed as brides. In the Roman Catholic Church, children receive their first Communion at about the age of nine, but are not confirmed until later. In some Anglican Churches this is also becoming the custom. In both Churches it is becoming more common to confirm young people at a later age, (perhaps over 16) than has been the case in the past (the age used to be nearer 11–13).

Little girl: 'Daddy, will the bishop move diagonally?'

The following story was told by a woman who late in life and very unexpectedly had what can only be called a 'conversion experience'. By no means all Christians have such an experience. Many are brought up in the Church and remain in it without ever having the sort of experiences Amy describes.

Amy's story

I was baptised when I was a baby. It was the done thing then. My mother went to Church but not my father. My Christian life stopped right there – at baptism. I never went to church again, although I think that at the back of my mind there was always the idea that somewhere there is a supreme being. I didn't have Jill, my daughter, baptised and never took her to church, but one day she told me over the phone that she had found faith through a House Church. Apparently she began to take her own children to a day nursery run by a fellowship group. All the women belonged to the House Church group, and they met in each other's homes. My daughter said to me, 'I realised that they all had something that I didn't.'

The next time I visited Jill she asked me to come to one of the meetings. I thought, 'My God, what's she got herself into?' I went in determined to get Jill out of it all. We went in to this huge room, full of people. One lady was about my age. They were seeing the film, *Faith Behind the Iron Curtain*. More than anything I wanted to run away. I kept on saying to myself, 'Why am I here?' But I couldn't show my daughter up. After the film some choruses were sung, and people prayed in tongues, while others gave the interpretation. Someone prophesied. It felt real, and I found myself saying, 'If this is worshipping God – it's good'. At the end I felt joyful – different. I went away full of thoughts I had never had before. When I got home,

I decided to find out more about the Christian faith. I knew that Liz across the road went to Church and asked her where she went. The bravest thing I ever did was to walk into that Church. (Only one other thing later was to be more difficult.) I sat next to Unis, whom I'd never met, and I said, 'I don't know what's going on, can you help me?' She helped me find my way through the service. It's a very hard thing to do, especially at my age, to go to a church and find yourself taking part in this service with its own particular language. You feel embarrassed because you don't know when to stand, sit or kneel. It's only after you've been a few times that you realise that no one minds about that sort of thing at all, and they're not looking at you.

Soon after this it was Easter. Jill came to see me and gave me the *Good News Bible*. I took it to bed and sat up reading it until 3 in the morning. I suddenly felt hungry for God's word. After I'd been going six times, Unis showed me how to go up to the altar and receive the blessing. Martin (the Vicar) asked me if I would like to be confirmed, and I said 'Yes'. I wasn't even sure at the time what it involved, but felt that it would help deepen my faith. I went to confirmation classes, and was confirmed $4\frac{1}{2}$ years ago. There were eight adults in the group and four children. Martin won't let anyone come who is not at least of secondary school age. He says that it's about taking responsibility for your own actions. What you need is experience of life — it's nothing to do with intelligence. There are some people who are brilliant intellectually, but you can see that they are just taking in the theory – they aren't making sense of it in their own lives – they don't *feel* it. No one confronts God without feeling terrified. Once I had committed myself to the Christian life, I could look in a mirror and know that a lot about me was rotten. I suddenly found that I was measuring myself by a different standard. More than anything I felt fear. I think I knew then that I was going to have to do something about my life – I couldn't ignore things which I had done previously. I found the worship reassuring. Martin told me that all adults who come to faith experience fear.

God asked for a lot in exchange. I now saw myself in a different, more honest light. There was one sin which I could not get rid of. I am divorced, and I hated my ex-husband. I kept on excusing myself to God, but knew I had to fight this one. I asked God for his help, and I talked a lot to Martin. One Thursday after morning Communion I made my confession to Martin. It was the hardest thing I ever had to do in my life, but since then I have known peace.

Confirmation was important to me now. I felt I belonged to the worldwide community of the Church. People I barely knew before gave me cards. At Confirmation each candidate nominates a sponsor, someone they feel has done most to bring them to Christ. I nominated Unis. I met the Bishop afterwards. I couldn't tell him I was divorced, but told him I was a grandmother. Afterwards I thought how silly it was to feel ashamed of being divorced. It was just pride – and I soon dealt with that.

Receiving Communion made a difference. For over a year I had been going up to receive a blessing. It's like always being the bridesmaid but never the bride! Taking the bread and wine does two things. It reminds me that Jesus died for me personally; and it reminds me that I am a member of a huge family.

I had heard 'speaking in tongues' and wanted the gift myself. I prayed a lot about it. It wasn't that I didn't find the usual Communion service helpful – I never receive the bread and wine without being aware of what Christ did for me. Then one day after I came home from St Augustine's I began praying in tongues. It made God very real – as though he were beside me. The gift of tongues is a gift of the Spirit. It is a wonderful experience for those who have it, but it does not make them in any way superior Christians. I can't really explain it. I find it very helpful when I'm upset and can't find the words. I never speak aloud in tongues unless I'm at a charismatic service. I know that some people think of it as mass hysteria, and I don't want to give offence. It's very personal and private.

At first I did not find in St Augustine's what I had found in the House Church. It seemed that doors had suddenly closed. Now I find God's word and his Holy Spirit there, joy and peace. Life is now more tranquil than it ever was. I think of St Augustine's, my local church, as the sort of 'main meal', and of the House Church as the icing on the cake.

Something to discuss and write about

1   Amy went through some very disturbing experiences which led her to the Christian faith. From her story, make a note of the experiences in which she felt the presence of God.

2   Why do you think Amy wanted to get Jill out of the House Church?

3   From what Amy says, what do you think were the differences between the House Church and St Augustine's?

4   Amy talks a lot about 'fear' and 'terror'. Also, Martin said that most adults coming to faith experience fear. What do you think they are afraid of?

5   Why was Amy afraid when she first went to St Augustine's?

6   Amy believes that her experiences were a result of a personal 'call' from God. How else could you explain her experiences?

7   If Amy was right, and she really did have an encounter with God, why should it be that some people experience such an encounter and some do not?

8   Why do you think that Amy only felt at peace after she confessed to her hatred of her husband? Why could she know no peace before?

Research

Find out more about House Churches.

Suggestions for coursework

Testing your knowledge
1 Attend a baptism service and write a report describing the ceremony. Remember to include these points: the denomination, the promises made; statements of faith made; other important words used; symbols; special clothes; special people present.
2 Attend a confirmation service (or use your own!). Write a letter to a friend describing the event.
3 What does the New Testament teach about baptism? (You will need a *Concordance* and a Bible).

Testing understanding
1 Explain the meaning of any *symbols* used at baptism. Write an illustrated talk which could be given to a class in your school.
2 Explain the meaning of the prayers, vows and statements of faith used at baptism.
3 Explain what Christians mean when they say that baptism is a sacrament.
4 Explain the various beliefs held about baptism by different Christians.
5 Design and make a baptism card for a baby to be baptised in a denomination of your choice. You should include:
   Illustrations which must have something to do with the meaning of baptism.
   A prayer or *poem* inside the card which could be read at the service. This prayer or poem must show that you understand what baptism means in that tradition.
Write a short passage to explain your choice of illustrations.
6 You have been asked to be a godparent and have said 'Yes'. Note the promises you will take on the baby's behalf, and explain carefully how you will try to carry out those promises.
7 You are *either* (a) about to be baptised, *or* (b) about to be confirmed.
   The priest/minister has told you that you may choose one New Testament reading for the service, and one hymn. Make a copy of the reading and hymn you have chosen, and carefully explain the reasons for your choice, explaining what the chosen reading and hymn have to say about the ceremony. (You will need: hymn books; a Bible; a *Concordance*.) You will need to think carefully about the *key words* which you want to look up in the *Concordance*, and in the index/list of first lines in the hymn books. You could write a short explanation about how you found your reading and hymn.
8 Attend *two* contrasting baptisms *or* *two* contrasting confirmation services. Explain the differences between the services and the reasons for these differences.

Tasks for evaluation
To 'evaluate' means to make a judgement about something on the basis of *argument* and *evidence*. Here are a number of questions which are often discussed and on which there is no agreement among all Christians. In making a judgement about these questions you need to consider:
Evidence
What does the Bible say about this?
   Is the teaching clear? Can it be interpreted in different ways?
   What does the tradition of the Church(es) say about it?
   What do Church leaders and leading Christians say about it?
Argument
Is the teaching of the Bible, traditions and leaders still *relevant* for today? (That is, has the world changed so much that Christians should take other things into consideration?)
   What arguments would *you* like to raise?
   Here are some of the questions you might discuss.
1   Should babies be baptised?
2   How seriously should, and do, people take the responsibilities of godparents? (survey needed)
3   Should people who don't go to Church have their children baptised?
4   The Society of Friends (Quakers) and the Salvation Army do not practise baptism at all, as they think it is unnecessary. Discuss this point of view.
5   Are 'born again' Christians in any sense 'better' or more genuine Christians than others? Is it important or necessary to have a 'conversion experience'?
6   At what age should people be confirmed?
7   Has there been a recent increase in adult baptisms? If so, why?

Marriage
The picture shows an ordinary Church of England marriage ceremony. The photograph would look much the same if it were taken in a Roman Catholic or Methodist or other Protestant Church. Marriage marks an important point in anyone's life – a time when they make a commitment to another person — a time when they set up a new home – and a time when many people begin to look forward to becoming parents.

Something to discuss and write about
1   Imagine that you were about to get married. Write a list of the ten things which you would be thinking or worrying about in the days leading up to the wedding.
2   Do you think that you would want to be married in Church? Explain the reasons for your answer.

When you discussed the first of these two questions, did you make a note of the serious promises you were about to make? This photograph was taken at the very beginning of the service. The bride and her father have just walked up the aisle to meet the groom and the best man. The priest is reading a long passage from the service book explaining what the marriage service is all about.

Activities

1   Here is the passage with some words missing. Working in small groups, try to fill in the missing words.

THE MARRIAGE
The bride and the bridegroom stand before the priest, and the priest says
We have come together in the presence of God, to witness the marriage of N and N, to ask his blessing on them, and to share in their joy. Our Lord Jesus Christ was himself a guest at a wedding in Cana of Galilee, and through his Spirit he is with us now.
The Scriptures teach us that marriage is a gift —— God in creation and a means of his grace, a —— mystery in which man and woman become one ——. It is God's purpose that, as husband and wife —— themselves to each other in love throughout their lives, —— shall be united in that love as Christ is —— with his Church.
Marriage is given, that husband and —— may comfort and help each other, living faithfully —— in need and in plenty, in sorrow and in ——. It is given, that with delight and tenderness they know each other in love, and, through the —— of their bodily union, may strengthen the —— of their —— and lives. It is given, —— they may have children and be blessed in —— for them and bringing them up in accordance with —— will, to his praise and glory.
In —— husband and wife belong to one another, and they —— a new life together in the community. It is a —— of life that all should honour; and it must —— be undertaken carelessly, lightly, or selfishly, but reverently, responsibly, and —— serious thought.
This is the way of life, —— and hallowed by God, that N and N are —— to begin. They will each give their consent to the ——; they will join hands and exchange solemn vows, and in —— of this they will give and receive a ring.
——, on this their wedding day we pray with them, that, —— and guided by God, they may fulfil his purpose —— the whole of their earthly life together.

2   Find the following words in the passage. Try to explain what they mean in context, and what they tell us about Christian ideas about marriage. Blessing (4), Joy (4), Grace (8), Holy mystery (8), One flesh (9), United (10), Comfort (12), Faithfully (13), Honour (20), Carelessly (21), Lightly (21), Selfishly (21), Reverently (22), Responsibly (22), Serious thought (22), Hallowed (23), Consent (24), Vow (25), Strengthened (27).

3   In your own words, explain FOUR reasons for marriage given in the text.

The promises

'Frank, will you take Jane to be your wife? Will you love her, comfort her, honour and protect her, and, forsaking all others, be faithful to her as long as you both shall live?'

Frank: I will.

The Vicar then asks Jane to make the same promise with regard to Frank.

Sequencing

The bride and groom both make several promises to each other. Here is the text of those promises, but the lines have been jumbled up. See how quickly you can rearrange the lines into the right order.

till death us do part
to have and to hold
for richer, for poorer
I, Jane, take you Frank,
according to God's holy law
from this day forward
to love and to cherish
and this is my solemn vow.
in sickness and in health
for better for worse.

I give you this ring
as a sign of our marriage:
with my body I honour you
all that I am I give to you
and all that I have I share with you
within the love of God
Father Son and Holy Spirit.

That which God has joined together
let not man divide.

The Roman Catholic service is very similar. There is a greater emphasis on children, who must be brought up within the Church. The Roman Catholic service is often followed by Mass.

The Orthodox service

There are two parts to the Orthodox ceremony. First there is the *Betrothal* as the bride enters the church. Promises are made, and rings are exchanged. Then there is the procession to the centre of the church. The procession stops in front of the table, on top of which are the Gospel, candles, and a cup of wine. Then the second part of the service begins.

The couple share a cup of wine, and as a sign that their marriage is to be endless, they walk around the altar three times.

'O Lord God, crown them with glory and honour.'

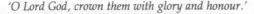

Suggestions for coursework

Knowledge and investigation

1 Attend a wedding and prepare a report or a talk to the class on what takes place.

2 Interview a priest or minister, and find out what beliefs he or she has about the importance of marriage.

3 You might discover something about attitudes to Christian marriage in your town or in Britain by;

(a) looking up national figures for marriage and second marriages in *Social Trends*.

(b) carrying out your own local surveys. You could try to find out what proportion of married couples married in church; what proportion of people who married in church go to church otherwise. Or you could carry out a similar survey in school about people's intentions when and if they marry.

Understanding

1 When people get married, they often produce an order of service for the wedding. Produce an order of service for a Christian wedding.

You will have to decide on (a) the hymns, (b) the readings, (c) special prayers, (d) music.

You will need: hymn books, a Bible, a *Concordance*, prayer book/service book/missal. You should choose two hymns, two readings (at least one of which must be from the Bible), one special prayer and two pieces of music.

Write a short passage explaining how you made your choices.

2 Put yourself in the place of the priest or minister taking a marriage service. Write a sermon which could be used for the occasion. (Remember to say what denomination you are — it may make a difference!)

Evaluation

1 Many people marry in church who rarely, if ever, go there otherwise. Are they hypocrites? Should priests and ministers be allowed to refuse to marry people who they feel cannot truly make promises in the name of the Trinity?

2 Is it realistic to expect young people to bind themselves to one person for the rest of their lives? Explain both sides of this argument.

3 Does the Christian marriage service represent many people's views on marriage today?

Four more sacraments

A reconciliation

1   Have you ever done something which has made you feel really guilty? (You don't have to tell the whole class what it was!) How did it make you feel?

2   When you do something wrong, does it help to 'get it off your chest' and tell someone? Why do you think people find this helpful?

3   If you do something which really hurts a friend badly, and you apologise, how might you feel if they:

    (a) just shrug it off as though it did not matter?

    (b) expect some sign that you mean it before your relationship returns to normal?

4   Is it better to 'sweep under the carpet' anything you do wrong, and never admit it? What might be the dangers of doing this? Look carefully at this picture. What words come into your mind?

Did you include words like 'talking', 'listening' 'still' 'quiet' 'peace'?

There are six people in the picture. Three of them are *priests* and the other three are *penitents*. A person is called a 'penitent' when they make their *confession* to a *priest*. After making their confession, they will receive the sacrament of *reconciliation*. The sacrament of penance is most common in the Roman Catholic and Orthodox Churches, but it is sometimes practised in Anglican and other Churches. The penitents tell the priest about the things which they feel they have done wrong. The priest listens carefully. In some churches you may have seen 'confessional' boxes where the penitent sits on one side of a division and the priest sits the other. These days, confession is often much less formal, and the priest and penitent will have a proper conversation or discussion about what has gone wrong. The priest

may give advice and try to help the penitent overcome their weakness, and put right what they have done wrong. The penitent makes a new commitment to start again and try not to make the same mistake another time. Sometimes, especially if he feels it will help the penitent, the priest will give them a penance to perform. This may be a matter of saying certain prayers, or it may involve saying sorry to a person they have offended.

More questions to discuss

1   When people go to church to make a formal confession, who are they confessing to? Do you think it is important to them that a *priest* hears their confession, or would a lay person do just as well?
2   It is believed by those who practise it, that confession is a *sacrament* through which *grace* is given. In what ways do you think the penitents in the photograph believe that God's grace will help them?

The sacrament of anointing the sick
'Through this holy anointing, may the Lord in his love and mercy help you with the grace of the Holy Spirit. May the Lord who freed you from sin save you and raise you up.'
Many Christians believe that through this sacrament they receive grace and strength. For some people this helps recovery, but for those who are dying it is believed that this sacrament brings final forgiveness for their sins before their death.

A Ukrainian Roman Catholic is ordained a priest. How would you describe the position he has taken up? What do you think it means?

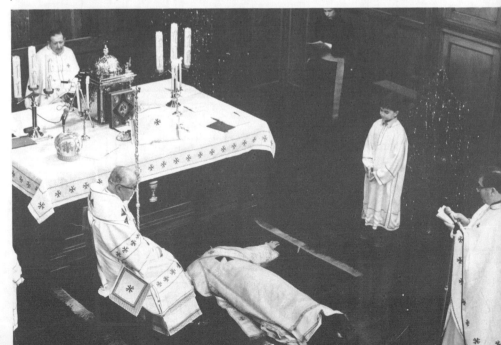

Holy Orders

In Chapter 1 you discovered that some Churches set apart men (and in a few cases women) as deacons, priests and bishops. It is believed that at their *ordination* these people receive the gift of the Spirit in a special way. This gives them *authority* in the Church. Deacons have the authority only to preach, baptise and assist at the Eucharist. Priests may also celebrate the Eucharist and forgive sins while only a Bishop may ordain priests and deacons, and confirm new church members. The bishop is also seen as an administrative figure who governs the Church. Only in a few branches of the Anglican Communion, are there women priests. Roman Catholic priests may not marry. In the Orthodox Church there are two sorts of priest – married, and unmarried (monks) – but only a monk may become a bishop.

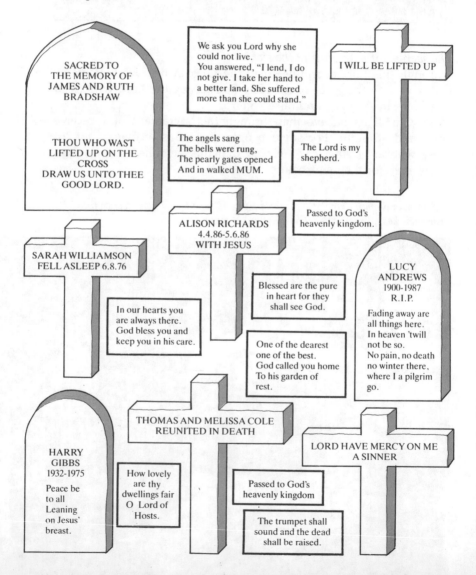

Burial

Activity

In the drawing are a number of gravestones with inscriptions. There are also some death notices from newspapers.   Working in pairs, do the following activities. (You will need a Bible and a *Concordance*.)

Draw up a chart across a double page in your work-book . . . like this.

Beliefs	Biblical reference	Meaning

In column 1. Write down briefly a list of beliefs about death which you have found on the tombstones and in the death notices. Many of these sayings come from the Bible, or refer to ideas found in the Bible. Using a *Concordance*, see how many of these references you can find. Write the reference in *column 2.* Finally in *column 3* write down what you think the saying means, and why it was chosen.

Research

Visit a cemetery yourself or with friends and do your own research into Christian ideas about death which are to be found there, using the following ideas.

Things to look for
(a) *Symbols* used, e.g. the shape of the stone.
(b) *Inscriptions* Have they changed over the years? Which are the most popular?
(c) You might be able to find graves of people belonging to different denominations. (There are some Roman Catholic and Orthodox burial grounds, but you will have to look for them.) Are there any differences between them?

A death in the family

Death usually causes unhappiness. You may believe that a friend or relative has gone to a 'better place', or that their death was a 'merciful release' from suffering, but the loss of that person in your everyday life is for a long time hard to live with.

Activity

1   Write down a list of what has to be done when a member of the family dies.
2   Make a list of people outside the family who can help, and say what sort of help you think they can give. You may be able to get some of these people to come into school to talk to your class.

The basis of Christian belief

You will have discovered by now that most, if not all, Christians believe that death is not the end — that life in some form continues after the physical body has ceased to function. Christians are not the only people who believe this, but the special points about Christian belief are based on the teaching of the New Testament.

Research

1   Read the following passages.
   John 11: 23–25 (Jesus)
   1 Corinthians 15: 12–58 (St Paul)

Make a list of the beliefs you discover in these two passages. You could list them under two headings:
   What will happen to the individual?
   What will happen at the end of time?

Discuss your reactions to the beliefs set out in these passages.

2   Make a collection of stories and accounts of events written in fairly modern times which suggest that the dead in some way live on (for example, the works of Rosemary Brown). Discuss your reactions to any such stories you may find.

Roman Catholic belief

Some of the most beautiful language in Christian prayer and worship is to be found in the services surrounding a person's death. It is common practice in the Roman Catholic Church to give a dying person their last Communion. This is called the *viaticum*, which means 'food for a journey'.

In the name of God, the almighty Father who created you,
In the name of Jesus Christ, son of the living God who suffered for you,
In the name of the Holy Spirit who was poured out upon you,
Go forth, faithful Christian.
May you live in peace this day,
May your home be with God in Zion.

Research

These words also appear in a famous Victorian poem written by Cardinal Newman, and set to music by Sir Edward Elgar. The poem is an imaginary account of the death of a Christian man, his experiences and visions as he goes on his last great journey. Try to find out what the poem is called and read at least part of it. Try to say in your own words what ideas Newman is expressing.

The funeral

At a Roman Catholic funeral the priest will usually be dressed in white, the colour which symbolises the resurrection. The body will have been sprinkled with holy water already. As in the Anglican service amongst others, he begins with the words 'I am the resurrection and the life'. (Where have you read those words before?) The priest says prayers expressing the hope that the soul will be happy for ever and will be raised with Christ at the Last Day. The Roman Catholic Church teaches that the soul does not go straight to 'heaven' but to a state called purgatory where it is purified. For this reason, it is common to pray for these souls. At every Mass a *requiem* is said:

Eternal rest grant unto them O Lord,
and let light perpetual shine upon them.

Research

Death and western culture
The words of the *requiem* have been set to music by many composers, and the settings are performed regularly in concert halls, even more than in church services. Find out the names of as many composers as you can who composed a requiem, and find pictures based on death and the Last Judgement. You could use this research as the basis for coursework. Here are some suggestions.

Music
1   Who composed a Requiem with *war* in mind? What text did he
include in his requiem apart from the traditional words of the Requiem
Mass? What message was he trying to get across to audiences about
death and about war?
2   Many composers wrote their Requiem near the end of their lives, or
for a special occasion. Find out about one who wrote letters explaining
what he felt about his requiem and why he was composing it. What was
he trying to say about death? How do you feel about his work?
3   One German composer wrote a Requiem with totally different words.
Find out who he was, where he got his text from, why he chose that
text and what message he was putting across about *Protestant* beliefs
concerning death.

Art
A number of artists have painted works on the theme of death and the
Last Judgement. Study one or more of these paintings and explain the
ideas conveyed in it/them. How far do you consider these beliefs are
still held by Christians today?

Orthodox belief

The Orthodox Church also says prayers for the dead, and asks *for*
the prayers of the dead. The Orthodox make no distinction between
the living and the dead in God's kingdom. All are members of God's
family, the only difference being that some exist in the spirit and not
in the body. As you might expect, the Orthodox service is full of
symbolism. The body is washed, dressed in new clothes and placed
in the coffin.

On the head is placed a strip of material on which are painted
pictures of John the Baptist, Jesus and Mary, the Mother of God. An
icon is placed in the hands. The body is covered with a cloth to show
that it is under the protection of Jesus.

In the Orthodox liturgy there is a beautiful hymn for the dead
called the Kantachion.

> *Give rest O Christ to all thy servants with thy saints*
> *Where sorrow and pain are no more, neither sighing, but life everlasting.*
> *Thou only art immortal, the creator and maker of man,*
> *And we are mortal born of the earth, and unto earth shall we return, all*
>   *we go down to the dust.*

Activities

1   Many elderly people especially are concerned that when they die
there will be enough money to pay for a 'respectable' funeral, and some
even take out an insurance policy which will pay for their funeral. Why
do you think that families often pay large sums for a funeral? Is it
important, and if so, for whom?

2 When a person dies, people tend to talk about them, and sometimes to write about them. What would you like to think that people could *honestly* say about you after you die? What would you like to be remembered for?

3 The man in the photo on p. 56 is caring for a grave. Why do you think he is doing this?

4 The following words are taken from the introduction to a funeral service.

In this place,
where through baptism and confirmation
Annie was admitted into the Church of Christ on Earth
We celebrate her admission into the Church of Christ in heaven.

I say 'celebrate'
For it was her wish that her death
Should not be surrounded with gloom and sadness
Which would be so untypical of her life.

Should a funeral service be a celebration for Christians? What do you think they can be said to be celebrating? When the actress Pat Phoenix died, a brass band came out of the Church playing 'When the Saints Go Marching In'. Do you think that this is better than a rather black, gloomy, solemn service?

5 Why do some people choose to be cremated while others still want a burial?

Suggestions for coursework

Testing knowledge – investigating

1 Make your own collection of inscriptions on gravestones or of death notices in the newspapers. Classify the types of sayings used, showing what beliefs they express.

2 Write an account of a Christian funeral service.

Testing understanding

1 Write a piece of work explaining one of the following:

(a) The meaning of Christian cemetery symbolism

(b) Christian understanding of death as illustrated through prayers and hymns commonly used at funeral services.

(c) The New Testament teaching about death.

2 Analyse a Christian poem about death (e.g. 'The Dream of Gerontius') explaining the concepts which appear in it. How common are such beliefs now?

3 Compare the *texts* of the Brahms Requiem and that of the Requiem Mass (as set to music by Mozart, Verdi, Berlioz, Lloyd-Webber, etc.). Explain the contrasting beliefs behind these texts and discuss to what extent each text is typical of modern Protestant and Catholic thinking.

4 Explain the meaning of ritual acts surrounding the dead in any two contrasting Christian traditions.

Testing evaluation
1   Does a belief in life after death make sense? If so, what form might this new life take?
2   Traditional Christian teaching suggests that not only do we live beyond the grave, but that we shall all be judged. If this is so, what difference should holding such a belief make to the believer's life?
3   If physical death is the end, what is the purpose of life?

Resources

Books
G. Read, J. Rudge and R. Howarth, *The Westhill Project, Book 4* (Mary Glasgow)
Brittain and Tredinnick, *Landmarks in Life* (Blackie)
Colinson and Miller, *Milestones* (Arnold)
J. R. Bailey, *Worship, Ceremonial & Rites of passage* (Schofield & Sims)
D. Atkinson, *Life and Death* (OUP)

Audio-visual aids
Slide centre   S1462 *Infant Baptism and Confirmation*
                S1463 *Dedication and Believers Baptism*
                S1466 *A Christian Wedding*
Videotext, *Aspects of Christianity*

Answers to the question on page 37
1   The priest reads the exorcism.
2   The baby's clothes are taken off and she is submerged in the water three times. (Before the baptism she faces west, but afterwards she faces east.)
3   The priest cuts the baby's hair as a sign that she is being dedicated to God.
4   The baby is anointed with oil. The priest makes the sign of the cross on her brow, eyes, nostrils, lips, ears, chest, hands, feet, saying each time 'The seal of the gift of the Holy Spirit'.
5   The baby is dressed in new white clothes and receives communion – the bread and wine – on a spoon. (In the Orthodox Church a child becomes a full member of the church as soon as she is baptised.)
6   The baby is given a special candle.

3 The Christian year

Objectives for Chapter 3

1 What you should KNOW.
The names of the important Holy Days of the Christian year: the ways in which these days are celebrated by Christians: some of the symbols and symbolic actions associated with these days: the traditional stories associated with these days.

2 What you should UNDERSTAND.
(a) *New words and technical terms*
Symbols; poems; allegory; myth; incarnation; Father; Son; Holy Spirit; festival; Holy Day; salvation; redemption.
(b) *People, writings and traditions*
(i) People: The way in which festivals and Holy Days keep alive the main events in the life of Jesus, and the important beliefs of the Church.
(ii) Writings: The importance of the New Testament as the foundation of Christian belief which is expressed on Holy Days.
(iii) Traditions: The traditional customs which have developed over the centuries in connection with Holy Days.
(c) *Belief*
The key Christian beliefs expressed at Holy Days (in particular, beliefs about the divinity and humanity of Jesus Christ).
(d) *Moral issues*
The reasons why important moral debates (e.g. poverty and peace) are especially associated with certain festivals.
(e) *Questions about the meaning of life*
The answers given to some of life's most difficult questions through the beliefs expressed through festivals: e.g. why do people suffer? what is our destiny? how can we be saved? what do we know about sin and evil?

3 What you should be able to DO.
Evaluate on the basis of evidence and argument, questions arising from the study of this chapter.

Remember

Anniversaries help us remember people and events. Some anniversaries are happy: e.g. a wedding anniversary, when most people celebrate the good years they have had together. Some anniversaries are solemn and remind us of sad times; e.g. Remembrance Day when we remember those who lost their lives in wartime.

Something to discuss and write about

This well-known rhyme was created in memory of an event in English history.

> Remember, remember the fifth of November,
> With gunpower, treason and plot;
> For we see no reason why gunpowder treason
> Should ever be forgot.

1 (a) What event is this rhyme about?
   (b) The poem tells us that we should never forget the fifth of November. Why?
2   See how many national anniversaries you can name. Make a list of them. What was important about the days they commemorate?
3   Make a list of all the 'anniversaries' remembered in your family. How are they remembered? Why are they remembered?
4   Do you think that any of the anniversaries you have read about or listed so far should be abolished? If so, explain why.

Religious 'anniversaries'

Nearly all religions have a calendar, or cycle, of anniversaries or special occasions. Christianity is no exception. These anniversaries are celebrated at about the same time every year and are held in memory of some special event in the past, usually associated with a special person. Remembering these events every year helps the members of the community keep alive their stories of important events in the past, while also teaching the stories to younger (or new) members of the community who may not be very familiar with them. Keeping these days alive also gives the community a chance to make a public demonstration of their faith.

In the Christian calendar, most of these anniversaries are festivals. Festivals are happy celebrations. But others are solemn times. These may be times of *fasting*, when instead of celebrating, often with special foods, members of the faith go without, or cut back on luxuries.

Brainstorm!

Working in groups of two or three, write down the names of as many Christian Holy Days, fasts and festivals as you can. You could check your list against the entries in a diary which includes Holy Days, or in the SHAP calendar of religious festivals, if the RS department has one.

You can work on the calendar as a group project while you are studying this chapter – but see that you get it finished by the time you go on to a new topic!

Advent

The Christian year begins with Advent.

Advent begins on the fourth Sunday before Christmas. The word Advent means 'coming', and it is the season of the year when Christians look forward to Christmas, the time of Jesus' 'coming' to Earth. Advent dates back to the sixth century AD.

Many Churches hold an Advent carol service. The readings, hymns, and symbolic actions at these services tell us a lot about Christian belief. The congregation arrives to a darkened church, and each person receives a candle. One by one the candles are lit, until the church is full of light. Some churches and homes have an Advent Crown with four candles. One candle is lit at the beginning of each of the weeks in Advent. The readings at the service are taken mostly from the Old Testament, usually from passages where the prophets tell of the coming of a saviour.

Two Advent readings

The Coming of the King

> The royal line of David is like a tree that has been cut down; but just as new branches sprout from a stump, so a new king will arise from among David's descendants.
> The spirit of the Lord will give him wisdom and the knowledge and skill to rule his people.
> He will know the Lord's will and have reverence for him, and find pleasure in obeying him.
> He will not judge by appearance or hearsay; he will judge the poor fairly and defend the rights of the helpless.

Wolves and sheep will lie together in peace,
And leopards will lie down with young goats.
Calves and lion cubs will feed together, and little children will take care of
them.

(*Isaiah 11:1–6*)

Questions

1 Isaiah is writing about a king to come. Who was to be this king's ancestor?
2 Write down two gifts which the king would be given by God.
3 Write down four things about this king's style of government, according to Isaiah.
4 What does the passage about the animals suggest about the state of the kingdom over which this king will rule?
5 Why do you think this passage has been chosen by some Churches to be specially read during Advent? (What connection does it have with the theme of Advent?)

The Forerunner

A voice cries out,
'Prepare in the wilderness a road for the Lord!
Clear the way in the desert for our God!'

(*Isaiah 40:3. Compare Mark 1:3 and Luke 3: 4–6.*)

This quotation from Isaiah is one verse of a much longer reading. In the Church of England, on the day when this passage from Isaiah is read, a special prayer called a *Collect* is said, which begins:

Almighty God,
who sent your servant John the Baptist
to prepare your people for the coming of your son. . . .

Questions

1 From these passages, what person is especially remembered during Advent?
2 Where else in the Bible can you find this passage from Isaiah?
3 This person is often called a 'forerunner'. Why?
4 What did he tell people to do?
5 Why do you think he is especially remembered during Advent?
6 You may have discovered by now that in churches where vestments and altar covers are used, the colour for Advent is purple. If you have not already done so, find out what the colour purple symbolises.
7 With reference to the last two questions, why do you think purple is worn during Advent?
8 Many other passages from the Old Testament like this one are read during Advent, Christmas and Easter – passages which tell of a king who will come to rule in the name of God. What does this suggest might be the beliefs of at least some Christians about the Old Testament?

Research

You will need an Alternative Service Book (Church of England). Find the Collect and the readings for Advent Sunday on page 422.

You will notice that *light* is a key word in some of these passages, but there is another theme which runs through them all. Can you spot what it is? (*Clue* – it refers to a very ancient Christian belief.)

Coursework on Advent hymns

Testing understanding and evaluation
You will need a collection of Hymn Books. Choose one Advent hymn. (Include a copy in your work.) Write a careful analysis of the hymn, explaining:

(a) what passages refer to the major beliefs expressed during Advent. (So, if you chose 'O come, O come Emmanuel', you will need to explain where the word Emmanuel comes from – don't forget your *Concordance*!; the idea that someone is expected – being asked to hurry up, in fact!; and the special use of the word Israel).

(b) Say whether you think this hymn is a suitable one for use at Advent. (Does it reflect the ideas connected with Advent?)

(c) If you chose a fairly old hymn, say whether you think that it still reflects what Christians believe. Is the language too difficult for most people to understand? Should new hymns be written for today? (Perhaps you could write one!)

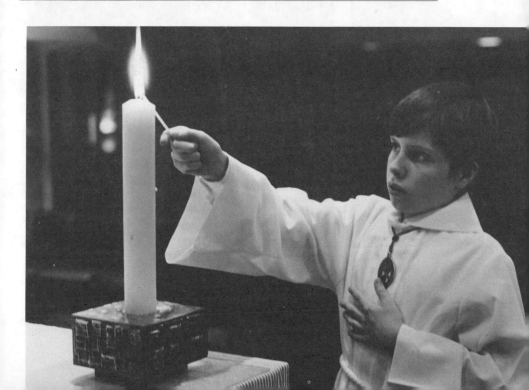

STOP!

Before you go on, check that you understand the following:

(a) Why *light* is an important theme during Advent.

(b) Why John the Baptist is remembered during Advent.

(c) Why certain passages from the Old Testament, especially from the prophet Isaiah are read in Church.

(d) Why the ancient belief in the 'second coming' of Jesus is often mentioned during Advent.

Christmas

First thoughts

In pairs, quickly write down ten things you associate with Christmas. Write a list on the board of all the ideas of the class. (At least one person should make a note, or an OHP transparency of this list, because you will need it later.)

Roman Catholic communities in London act out the traditional Christmas story.

1   2

You are about to answer some questions.

LEAVE SOME SPACE AT THE BOTTOM OF EACH ANSWER – YOU MAY WANT TO WRITE MORE LATER!

Picture quiz – Test Your Knowledge

Look at picture 1 – this tells part of a famous story.
1   What character is being played by the little boy?
2   How did this person (and his companions) come to be involved in the story?
3   Why do you think it is important that these people were told of Jesus' birth? What does this say about Jesus'?
4   Where in the Bible would you find this version of the story?

Look at picture 2 – it tells another version of the same story. See how much of the story you can remember just by studying the picture.
1   In (a) which town and (b) which country did the events dramatised in this picture first take place?
2   A man, a woman and a baby are under what looks like a shelter. Who are they?
3   According to the story, what was very unusual about the relationship between the man and woman in the 'shelter'?
4   Three people have their backs to the camera. Who are they, and how did they come to be present?
5   What three things should these people be holding, and why did they bring those particular gifts?
6   What 'warning' did these three people receive after their visit? What was the reason for that warning, and what was its result?
7   Where in the New Testament can you find the story as it appears in this picture?
8   What would you say are the main differences between the people represented in this picture, and the visitors in picture 1?

Believe it or not . . .

The story of the events leading up to, and following on Jesus' birth is one of the best-known in the world. The story makes the following claims:

- Jesus was not conceived in the ordinary way. His mother was a virgin, who in some way became pregnant by the action of the *Holy Spirit* (Luke 1:28–32; Matthew 1:18–20).
- Jesus was the *Son of God* (Luke 1:35).
- Jesus was born in poverty.
- Jesus was to be the *Saviour* of humanity (Luke 2:11; Matthew 1:21).
- His birth was announced by angels (Luke 2:8–14; Matthew 1:20–21).
- Jesus was born in Bethlehem, when Herod the Great was King of the Jews, and Augustus was Roman Emperor (Luke 2:1; Luke 1:5; Matthew 2:1).
- Jesus' mother was called Mary and her husband was called Joseph (Matthew 1:18).
- When Jesus was born, a star appeared in the East (Matthew 2:2).
- King Herod tried to kill Jesus, and in so doing, killed many babies in Bethlehem (Matthew 2:16).

Something to discuss and write about

1 The statements on p. 67 fall roughly speaking into two types. Can you explain what these two types of statement are?

2 Some Christians when they study the New Testament, talk about 'The Jesus of History' and 'The Christ of Faith'.
What do you think they mean by these expressions?

3 Perhaps you labelled the statements something like 'historical' and 'faith' or 'belief'. Some of the statements make historical claims, i.e. they make statements of fact, which could possibly be proved or disproved. But other statements state a *belief*, and can never be proved or disproved using historical evidence. They say what Matthew or Luke, and the early Christians believed about Jesus. It would be difficult to prove in any way whether these statements are 'true' or not. Try to list the statements under two headings; *Historical statements* and *Faith statements*. Discuss your choice with your partner / group.

4 Look at the statements you have labelled as 'historical'. The writers of the Gospels clearly see these as statements of fact. Which ones do you think could be proved to be (more or less) accurate to your satisfaction (say how!)? Which ones would you have great difficulty in believing, and why?

5 Matthew in particular often quotes from the Old Testament prophets while telling the birth story. Before writing down the prophecy, he might write:

In this way what the prophet . . . had said came true.

or

This was done to make what the Lord had said through the prophet come true.

What does this suggest that Matthew and the early Christians believed about the Old Testament? Find out if Christians today still believe this.

Credo

I believe . . . in Jesus Christ, his only Son our Lord, who was conceived of the Holy Ghost, born of the virgin Mary. . . .

(from the Apostles' Creed)

We believe . . . in one Lord Jesus Christ, The only begotten Son of the Father. . . . Who for us men and for our salvation came down from heaven, and was incarnate by the Holy Ghost of the Virgin Mary, And was made man.

(from the Nicene Creed)

Christian belief explained

New words
sin; redemption; restoration; incarnation; Jesus; Son of God

The meaning of Christmas for Christians can be summed up in the word *incarnation*, which means, 'in the flesh'.

All forms of Christianity emphasise the concept of *salvation* very strongly. You will often see notices outside churches claiming that Jesus Christ is our *Saviour*. But what is he supposed to be saving people from? The Christian answer would be, 'from themselves, and from their sin'. The argument goes like this:

1 Human beings were meant to be like God. That is what the Book of Genesis means when it says that 'man was made in the image of God'. Because human beings were so special, the world was entrusted to their care.

2 But human beings 'fell from Grace' and developed a tendency to sin. This state is known as 'the Fall'. As a result, they lost their image of God and their destiny. The story about Adam and Eve is an attempt to explain that fall. The Old Testament shows the human race moving further and further away from God, in spite of the many attempts by the Prophets to call them back to the path they were intended to follow.

3 Humans had become so far removed from God, that it was impossible for them to re-establish their relationship with him by their own efforts. It was as though the human race owed a debt to God which could never be paid. The only person who has the means to pay that debt was God himself, and this is exactly what he did. He provided his son as a sacrifice which 'paid off the debt', and made it possible for the human race to be restored to the relationship which they had with God in the beginning, rather than be lost for ever.

4 Jesus was God's instrument in restoring people to their full humanity – or making it possible for them to be restored. In order to do this, he had to lead a fully human life in order to show people what 'full humanity' was like. In this sense he was a model for all people to copy, he emphasised the need for justice, equality and peace. This is why many Christians now say that salvation is not something for the individual but for the whole human race. None can be fully human until all are fully human, because as long as there are glaring injustices and inequality in the world, there is a lack of humanity in all who allow this situation to continue.

Revision

A Look back at the questions on p. 67 and the answers you gave. Is there anything you could now add to your answers? If so, write it down.
B Read carefully, and answer the questions on, the words of this famous Christmas carol, 'Christians Awake'.

1 CHRISTIANS, awake! salute the happy morn,
   Whereon the Saviour of the world was born;
   Rise to adore the mystery of love,
   Which hosts of angels chanted from above:
   With them the joyful tidings first begun
   Of God incarnate and the Virgin's Son.

2 Then to the watchful shepherds it was told,
   Who heard the angelic herald's voice, 'Behold,
   I bring good tidings of a Saviour's birth
   To you and all the nations upon earth:
   This day hath God fulfilled his promised word,
   This day is born a Saviour, Christ the Lord.'

3 He spake; and straightway the celestial choir
   In hymns of joy, unknown before, conspire;
   The praises of redeeming love they sang,
   And heaven's whole orb with Alleluias rang:
   God's highest glory was their anthem still,
   Peace upon earth, and unto men good will.

4 To Bethlehem straight the enlightened shepherds ran,
   To see the wonder God had wrought for man,
   And found, with Joseph and the blessèd Maid,
   Her Son, the Saviour, in a manger laid:
   Then to their flocks, still praising God, return,
   And their glad hearts with holy rapture burn.

PART 2

5 O may we keep and ponder in our mind
   God's wondrous love in saving lost mankind;
   Trace we the Babe, who hath retrieved our loss,
   From his poor manger to his bitter Cross;
   Tread in his steps, assisted by his grace,
   Till man's first heavenly stage again takes place.

6 Then may we hope, the angelic hosts among,
   To sing, redeemed, a glad triumphal song:
   He that was born upon this joyful day
   Around us all his glory shall display;
   Saved by his love, incessant we shall sing
   Eternal praise to heaven's almighty King.

J. Byrom

Now write down any words or phrases from the carol which mean:
(a)   That Jesus was born into a humble household.
(b)   That Jesus was born into a poor household.
(c)   That the news of Jesus' birth was first told to the poor.
(d)   That Mary was privileged to be Jesus' mother.
(e)   That Jesus was God in the form of a man.
(f)   That Jesus was born in order that the human race might be saved.
(g)   That Jesus was to guide and care for his people.
(h)   That Jesus is a King.

Christmas traditions and customs

Look again at the list of things which your class said they associated with Christmas. Go though the list and discuss which of these things you believe has a directly *Christian* meaning.

You probably realised that many of the most popular Christmas traditions have little to do with Christianity at all. Some of the customs did not have their origins in Christian tradition but have been given a Christian interpretation in more recent years. The very date of Christmas was not fixed until the fourth century AD. No one actually knows at what time of the year Jesus was born, but in the West his birth came to be celebrated on 25 December, near the time of the winter solstice – the point in the year when the days begin to get longer again, and people in the northern hemisphere look forward to the return of the sun after the dark days of winter.

Why do you think that the time of the winter solstice was regarded as a suitable time to celebrate the birth of Jesus?

At this time of the year, the Romans used to hold a mid-winter festival called Saturnalia. Food, drink, parties and the giving of presents were all features of this festival. Also, people used to decorate their houses with winter greenery, like laurel and holly. Once Europe became Christian, it was an easy matter for people to keep their old customs, but give them a Christian meaning. So the festivities of Saturnalia became celebrations held in honour of the birth of Christ. The giving of presents was explained as being in memory of the gifts given to Jesus by the wise men.

Coursework

All the coursework assignments suggested here may also be used as either display work or as Assembly presentations, which should be informative to other people in the school.

1   One popular Christmas symbol, especially in central Europe, is the *Christingle*.

(a) Find out as much as you can about the Christingle and its history. Draw or make one (if you are submitting this is as a piece of coursework, take a photograph of it to include with your work.)   (K)

You could use this work as the basis of a school assembly at Christmas.

(b) Prepare a talk about the Christingle, explaining what all its symbols mean, and what they tell us about the meaning of Christmas.   (U)

(c) What do you think are the advantages of using symbols to get across a religious message? Do you think there are any dangers in using symbols in this way?   (E)

2   Find out about the origins of the Christmas crib which can still be found in many churches and homes. Make a crib for display in your classroom, or the school hall, etc.

(a) Write a talk about the crib, its origins and history.   (K)

(b) Explain *either* the importance in Christian teaching of the characters represented in the 'crib', *or* why you can't find all the characters in any one version of the Christmas story in the Bible.   (U)

(c) Some Christians do not approve of the practice of representing characters in the Bible in the form of statues. Do you think there are any dangers in this practice?   (E)

3   Collect as many Christmas cards as you can. Make a collage of

(i) pictures which you think *do* have a direct connection with the Christmas story, and

(ii) pictures which have little or nothing to do with the Christian meaning of Christmas.

(a) Write a piece about the origins and history of the Christmas card.   (K)

(b) Explain how the Christian message is passed on through the pictures and symbols on the 'religious' cards.   (U)

(c) 'Giving cards and presents to people at Christmas has become a matter of routine. No one really means anything by it any more. It's just something you do. It's about time they stopped the custom – it's more trouble than it's worth.' Give your reasons for agreeing or disagreeing with this statement.   (E)

Christmas and caring

Christmas is traditionally a time for giving, and thinking of others.

Group work

1   Make a list of all the charities which you associate with Christmas. You may have seen them collecting at stations, or carol singing. They may call at your house, or sell flags. You may have held events in school

at Christmas raising money for charity. With what sort of people are these charities mainly concerned in your experience?
2   Are any of these charities specifically Christian? If so, write to them (including an s.a.e.) and ask for information about the charity, and how its work is inspired by the Christian message. Make a collage of your material.

Crisis at Christmas
One charity which is particularly associated with Christmas is 'Crisis at Christmas', a charity which deals with the needs of the homeless. Here is an extract from one of their pamphlets.

The Open Christmas
The charity's direct contribution to the single homeless is the Open Christmas held annually from 23 to 29 December. For this, a large disused building such as a redundant church or warehouse is taken over. In it are provided meals, entertainment and day and night shelter for several hundred homeless people. The project includes a medical centre, staffed 24 hours a day by qualified first aiders with doctors providing daily surgeries. There is a clothes store from which all the guests are provided with clean and warm clothes. Logistical problems include obtaining sufficient mattresses and blankets for the nights, setting up a kitchen, providing toilet and shower facilities and finding nearly a thousand capable volunteers, who work in shifts to prepare, run and clear up the Open Christmas.

If you wish to find out more about Crisis at Christmas and the projects it supports please telephone or write to the address below. Donations of money and offers of help in kind are welcome throughout the year.

Crisis at Christmas
212 Whitechapel Road
London E1 1BJ

Telephone: 01 377 0489

Charity number 266533

Activities – discussion
1   Think of a connection between homelessness and the Christmas story. Why is caring for the homeless an especially appropriate thing for Christians to do at Christmas?
2   Many people give up their traditional family Christmas to work with 'Crisis' in their 'Open Christmas' shelters. Why might some Christians argue that this way of keeping Christmas is more in keeping with the Christian message than the usual celebrations?
3   Find other passages in the Gospels which suggest that Christians should be concerned with the homeless.

Do they know it's Christmas?

> It was coming to the end of 1984 . . . I went home in a state of blank resignation and switched on the television. I saw something that placed my worries in a ghastly new perspective.
>
> The news report was of famine in Ethiopia. From the first seconds it was clear that this was a horror on a monumental scale. The pictures were of people who were so shrunken that they looked like beings from another planet. The camera wandered amidst them like a mesmerised observer, occasionally dwelling on one person so that he looked directly at me, sitting in my comfortable living room surrounded by the fripperies of modern living which we were pleased to regard as necessities.
>
> (Bob Geldof, *Is That It?*, Sidgwick & Jackson, and Penguin)

It was this television broadcast which moved Bob Geldof to start one of the most ambitious moneyraising activities for the poor ever known. He called together all the great names in the pop music business, who gave their services free, and they made what was to become the number 1 hit *Do they know it's Christmas?* under the group name of Band Aid.

Bob Geldof tells of his efforts to sell the record . . .

I began with a round of TV, radio and newspaper interviews. The mouth that had got me into trouble so often now talked about *the simple idea of personal responsibility*. The thing I first groped with back in the Simon Community in Dublin now became clear. 'Everyone can do something. No matter what you do, you can do something. Use your talent, your circumstances, anything. There are millions dying in agony. How many will you let die in your living rooms before you act? Even if you hate the song, buy it and throw it away.'

The grand culmination of Band Aid was the Live Aid performance of non-stop music which was broadcast all over the world on 13 July 1985. Geldof recalls how people approached him in the street on his way home from Wembley on that day. . . .

Some cried, 'Oh Bob, oh Bob,' not sneering, not uncontrollable, *just something shared and understood*. 'I know', was all I could say. I did know. I wasn't sure what had happened in England, or everywhere else, but I knew. Somehow something had gone right. *Cynicism and greed and selfishness had been eliminated for a moment*. It felt good. *A lot of people had rediscovered something in themselves.*

Activities – discussion

A Read carefully the words in italic. Talk and write about your reactions to and feelings about these sections and their meaning.
B Write a poem which you think someone involved in Band Aid might have written at Christmas to accompany the picture and caption.

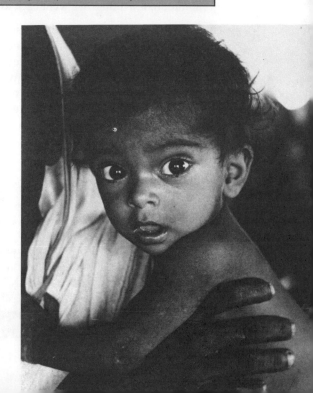

'He looked directly at me.'

Peace at Christmas

Christmas 1914
This is an extract from *Old Soldiers Never Die* by Frank Richards.

On Christmas morning we stuck up a board with 'A Merry Christmas' on it. The enemy had stuck up a similar one. Two of our men then threw their equipment off and jumped on the parapet with their hands above their heads. Two of the Germans had done the same and commenced to walk up the river bank, our men going to meet them. They met and shook hands and then we all got out of the trench. Buffalo Bill rushed into the trench to try and prevent it, but it was too late; the whole of the company were now out, and so were the Germans. He had to accept the situation, and soon he and the other officers climbed out too.

We mucked in all day with one another. They were Saxons and some of them could speak English. By the look of them, their trenches were in as bad a state as our own. One of their men, speaking in English, mentioned that he had worked in Brighton for some years and was fed up with this damned war and would be glad when it was all over. We told him that he wasn't the only one that was fed up with it. The German Company Commander asked Buffalo Bill to accept a couple of barrels of beer and assured him that they would not make his men drunk. He accepted the offer with thanks and a couple of their men rolled the barrels over and we took them into our trench. The German officer sent one of his men back to the trench, who appeared shortly after carrying a tray with bottles and glasses on it. Officers on both sides clinked glasses and drank one another's health. Buffalo Bill had presented them with a plum pudding just before. The officers came to an understanding that the unofficial truce would end at midnight. At dusk we went back to our respective trenches.

1   Why do you think the killing stopped on Christmas Day?
2   What do you think is the likelihood of this sort of truce taking place on Christmas Day in a modern war?
3   'Jesus is the Prince of Peace who came to teach men to live as brothers, loving their enemies, not killing them. If Christian men stop fighting on Christmas Day because they believe this, it is hypocritical of them to fight on any other day.' How would you respond to this statement?

Coursework suggestions

1   Write a School Assembly for Christmas. You might *either*:
   (a) Select traditional carols and readings written by someone else. In this case, you should accompany your script (for coursework purposes) with a detailed explanation as to why you chose those particular readings and carols.   (K/U) *Or*:
   (b) Write your own material. In this case you should include
(i) some factual information about Christmas (perhaps its origins; the Christmas story; customs, etc.)   (K)

(ii) some explanation as to the meaning of Christmas for Christians.   (U)

(iii) some discussion of a controversial point (e.g. has Christmas become too commercialised? Is the story historically true? etc.   (E)

2   Write your own nativity play for today, bringing out the message of Christmas.   (U/E)

3   Write your own Christmas carol, bringing out the Christian message of Christmas (it will be assessed on the words, not the music).   (U/E)

4   Find out about the way Christmas or Epiphany is celebrated in another country, and explain the difference in customs and traditions.   (K/U)

From Lent to Whitsun

Lent

The 40 days before Easter are known as Lent, and the last seven days of Lent are known as Holy Week.

The story associated with Lent is of how Jesus went into the wilderness for 40 days and 40 nights to prepare for his ministry, and was tempted by the Devil (Mark 1:12–13; Luke 4:1–13).

In the early days of the Church, this season became a time of *penitence*. It was especially a time when new converts to the faith prepared themselves for their baptism which would take place at Easter. As part of this preparation, they fasted (they would have had one meal a day, but no luxuries like fish or meat) for the full 40-day period. It soon became the custom for the whole Church to join them in this fast and preparation.

It is still possible to find Christian communities which fast during Lent, and many Christians still keep the practice of 'giving up' some luxury during Lent and giving the money to charity. Many Churches run special prayer meetings and study-groups during Lent, for it is above all a time when Christians today reflect on their faith and their lives. It is a solemn time when many Churches display the colour purple, or even sackcloth, and the hymns tend to be serious and mournful.

There are a number of especially important days during Lent and Holy Week.

Shrove Tuesday This is better known as 'Pancake Day'. It is the last day before Lent begins, and in the past people would make pancakes to use up all the rich foods which they would not be eating during Lent. People went to Church on Shrove Tuesday to confess their sins and to be 'SHRIVEN' – that is, forgiven – hence the name SHROVE TUESDAY.

Ash Wednesday is the first day of Lent. It takes its name from the custom of making a mark with ash on the foreheads of worshippers who attend church on that day.

Coursework suggestions

1 Find out about the origins of Lent, and explain the importance of some of the traditions associated with it in the past.   (K/U)
2 Find out about a community or individuals who still take the Lent fast seriously. Why do they regard fasting as important?   (K/U)
3 Carry out a survey in your school to find out:
  (a) How many people give up something for Lent.
  (b) How many of those who *do* give up something know where the tradition comes from?
  (c) The reasons people offer for giving up something for Lent.
  (d) How many people consider that it is a good idea to have a specially fixed time when people are encouraged to think about the way they are living their lives, and try to change things they don't like about themselves?
  What conclusions, if any, do you draw from your survey?   (K/U/E)

Holy Week

Holy Week is the most solemn week in the Christian year, and is in memory of the last week of Jesus' life on Earth. Many of the days in Holy Week have a special importance in Britain and other parts of the world.

Palm Sunday Christians remember the entry of Jesus into Jerusalem on a donkey. During Church services everyone is given a palm cross

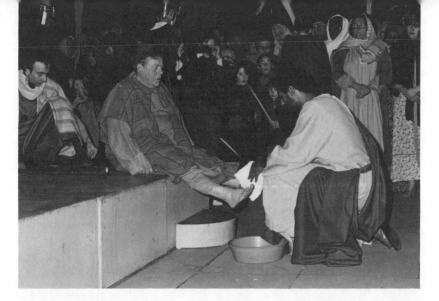

which they keep for the next year. Many Churches have processions, with members of the congregation waving palm branches (Mark 11:1–10; Luke 19:28–38.

Maundy Thursday On the last Thursday of his life, Jesus ate the Last Supper with his disciples. John's Gospel tells us that he washed his disciples' feet, giving them a new *commandment*; 'As I have loved you, so you must love one another.' The Latin for the word commandment is *mandatum*, and this is how Maundy Thursday gets its name.

To this day, the Pope washes the feet of twelve people on Maundy Thursday, and the same ceremony is carried out in many Churches. In previous centuries, the English monarch used to do the same thing (Mark 14:12–31; Luke 22:7–34; John 13:1–17).

Good Friday On this day Christians remember the death of Jesus on the Cross. Many Churches hold public acts of witness, processing with a cross. In Jerusalem itself, the city where Jesus died, processions last from morning to evening, as pilgrims follow the traditional route taken by Jesus as he carried his cross from the judgement hall to the place of execution.

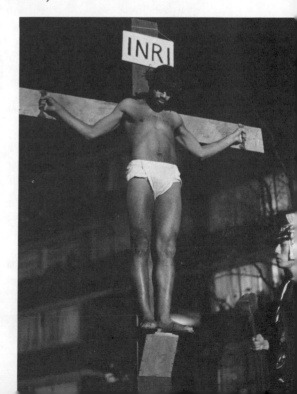

Credo

He suffered under Pontius Pilate,
was crucified, dead and buried.

(from the Apostles' Creed)

And was crucified also for us, under Pontius Pilate.
He suffered and was buried.

(from the Nicene Creed)

Coursework suggestions

Study carefully the pictures on pages 78–9.
Answer these questions. (Knowledge)
1   Find out about and describe the event in the life of Jesus which is being acted out in each of these photographs.
2   Answer these questions.
(a) What names are given to the three days on which Christians remember the events in these three pictures?
(b) What custom is carried out by the Queen instead of the activity in the second picture?
(c) If there were a fourth picture in the series, explain what you think it might look like. (You may draw it if you wish.)
(d) What special name is given to the week in which these events are remembered?
(e) Name one symbol in each picture.
(f) Find all the places in the Bible where you can read the accounts of these three events. Make a note of the references.
3   Answer these questions. (Understanding)
(a) Look at the first and second pictures. Explain carefully the meaning and purpose of Jesus' actions in these photographs.
(b) Look at your answer to 2 (d). Why is this name given to this week?
(c) Look at the third picture. If someone were to say to one of the actors, 'Why didn't Jesus use his power to save himself?', what answer might he give?
(d) Imagine that you were one of the people taking part in the Passion Play. Write an article for the local paper explaining why you were taking part, and why this sort of public activity was important to you.
4   Answer these questions. (Evaluation)
(a) What do you think the death of Jesus has to teach the world in the 1980s?
(b) Why do you think so many Christians make a point of acting out the events in the last week of Jesus' life? (e.g. Palm Sunday processions; processions with the cross; making Easter Gardens, etc.) If they find this sort of thing helpful, why do you think this should be?

(c) Imagine that you were living in the flats overlooking the street in the first and third pictures on pp. 78–9. What would be your reaction to what was going on below?

Easter Day This is the most important day in the Church's year. On Easter Day Christians celebrate the resurrection of Jesus from the dead. Churches are decorated in gold and white; the music, which had been so sorrowful during Lent, is now happy and triumphant. In many Churches, the great Paschal Candle is lit at midnight, as Easter Day begins, and smaller candles are set alight and given to the congregation.

The Resurrection story

Read the stories of the Resurrection in Luke 23:50–56; 24:1–12, 13–35, 36–48.

Easter at the Holy Sepulchre

A visitor to Israel remembers the celebration of Easter in the Orthodox tradition in the Church of the Holy Sepulchre in Jerusalem.

You know what it's like in a big city round about 8 or 9 o'clock when the shops are all open, and the lights are all on – well, Jerusalem was just like that but at 11 p.m. The shops were not open, but in the Christian quarters light seemed to be coming from everywhere. People were walking through the streets in their summer clothes towards the great Church – the atmosphere was festive but at the same time there was a feeling of expectancy in the air – almost of tension.

We arrived at the church in good time – we had been told it would be crowded even more than usual this year because, unusually, the Eastern and Western dates for Easter fell on the same day. Just inside the church is a large slab of marble, traditionally the spot where Jesus was laid out after he was taken from the cross. People were kneeling on the floor and throwing flowers over it and kissing it. All around us were sitting elderly women in black. They had been there on Friday when we came – and earlier today. Their faces were a study. Some of them held rosaries – some were crying – they were all murmuring prayers quietly. It was as though they had suffered with Jesus all through his crucifixion and were now willing the resurrection to happen. I wish I could have read their minds – or spoken their language so that I could ask them what it meant to them to be there, at the very spot where Jesus was said to have died, and where in the tradition of the Orthodox Church he was buried and first appeared to Mary Magdalene.

The chaos in the church had shocked us at first. People were pushing and shoving – one little nun was so determined to get into the Holy Sepulchre itself that she was elbowing everyone out of the way! But then we realised that it was not our Christian principles that were being offended but our English concept of 'good manners', which many Eastern Europeans do not bother with. Pushing and shoving when getting onto buses and trains is quite frowned upon in England as being 'not quite nice' – but as anyone who has been to Italy or Greece knows, it is perfectly accepted elsewhere. It reminded me how much so-called 'Christian' behaviour depends on local culture and custom.

There were processions going in all directions – the Syrians from the right, the Armenians from the left, and a crocodile of Franciscans, doing their best to look dignified in the face of chaos, processing in orderly fashion straight through the middle of the Syrian procession which had got itself into a terrible muddle! The whole church – which seemed to me to be more like a collection of churches and chapels under one roof – was alive with noise, bustle and colour. It was one of those really emotional occasions which bring tears to your eyes because you are aware of being there – of being part of it.

Just behind the Holy Sepulchre is a little cell – almost underground – where an old Coptic monk sits all day selling candles and saying prayers with people who go in. We bought candles and went to find a seat in the main part of the church which is run by the Greek Orthodox. It was a bit late to find a seat, but we managed to stand quite near the front behind two lovely Greek women who lit our candles from theirs. I found that really moving. We didn't speak each other's language but we knew that we were there for the same reason and so we could communicate with smiles and hand gestures. 'English?' they asked. We nodded. Then they lit the candles. There was something magic about it – the great candelabras were let down from the dome and young men in richly embroidered red robes sent them back in a blaze of light. In other parts of the church too, flickers of light appeared, and the hitherto hushed murmurs of the congregation rose once more to fever pitch. The word went round: 'The Patriarch's coming'. We stood on tiptoe, craning our necks following everyone else's gaze.

And sure enough the Patriarch did arrive – a majestic figure in black with a train of monks and Priests. He sat, and one by one they processed before him kissing his hand. After about 10 minutes, we caught him rather unobtrusively pulling up his sleeve about an inch and stealing a glance at his watch. My friend giggled. I kicked her. Then came the moment we had been waiting for. The whole Church rose and the procession began. We were miles behind everyone else, but news of what was happening in front was being passed back in every language you could think of. 'They're going up the stairs to the site of Calvary now. . . .' 'They're coming down the other side. . . .' 'They're going round to the Sepulchre.' And then it happened – the whole building seemed to vibrate with the great cry for which the women in black had held vigil for two days. '*Christos anesté*', cried the priests from the Holy Sepulchre, on finding that the icon of Christ placed there on Friday had now gone. And all around us people greeted each other, '*Christos anesté*' – 'Christ is risen!' '*Christos anesté*' chattered one of our Greek friends. I couldn't remember the response in Greek, but I shook her hand, and with equal enthusiasm cried, 'He is risen indeed.'

> Yesterday I was buried with Thee, O Christ. Today I arise with Thee in Thy resurrection. Yesterday I was crucified with Thee. Glorify me with Thee, O Saviour, in Thy kingdom.

The importance of Easter

Easter is the most important of all Christian festivals. Christians see the Resurrection as the greatest sign given by God to show his love for the human race. Jesus was not raised simply for his own sake, but as a sign that all who believe in him will also be raised. It was a sign to everyone that death is not the end.

Credo

On the third day he rose again.   (*from the Apostles' Creed*)

Easter customs

An ancient tradition is the giving of Easter eggs. The egg is itself the symbol of new life and many communities still keep the custom of rolling eggs down the hill as a reminder of how the stone was rolled away from Jesus' tomb (Mark 16; Luke 24).

Easter marches

It has become the custom for many Christians to join anti-nuclear rallies over the Easter weekend. Christians from all denominations march together in protest against the installation of nuclear weapons in Britain, largely in American bases. These Christians appeal to the teaching of the Gospel in support of their action, while other Christians equally criticise what they are doing. Read this article from the *Methodist Recorder*, 1984.

Why we're campaigning this Easter

This Holy Week many Christians are making a pilgrimage from the Cruise missile base at Greenham Common, via several more bases to Lakenheath in Suffolk, the largest USAF base in Europe and home of the F1-11 nuclear bombers. Here there will be a major peace festival on Easter Monday.

Is it wrong for Christians to campaign for nuclear disarmament in Holy Week? Mr John Gummer, chairman of the Conservative Party and a Christian, says it is. He has already criticised Christian CND, one of the organisations sponsoring the pilgrimage, for using a major festival of universal Christian significance to promote a particular contentious issue in a one-sided way.

In this country the Churches have for so long been largely part of the social and political establishment that we tend to forget how radically, publicly and controversially Jesus challenged the established values of his day. In particular, on the first Palm Sunday he confronted the authorities, the Zealots, and popular messianic expectations with a radically new concept of leadership.

In entering Jerusalem not on a warhorse but a donkey he signalled that true leadership lies in the ability not to exercise superior force, but to bring peace – not just the absence of fighting, but biblically 'Shalom' of which he saw himself as the fulfilment.

Today, as then, rulers believe in the value of violence, and Jesus represents all innocent victims of violence.

Nuclear governments in particular believe that superiority in weapons of mass destruction is essential to good leadership in the world. In any war, the killing of innocent people is possible. In nuclear war it is inevitable and deliberate. Nuclear deterrence means planning for the death of millions of innocents, including fellow Christians, on both sides.

For innocents in the Third World the nuclear holocaust has, in a sense, already begun, since the nuclear powers have decided that it is more important to spend money on the arms race than on preventing widespread death from malnutrition. They have, however, given the Third World nuclear technology. Under the 1968 Non-proliferation Treaty this was supposed to be for civil purposes, but some Third World rulers use it to make nuclear bombs. There is a stock of them, for example, in the Middle East, and Iraq's recent use of nerve gas shows how frighteningly tenuous is the inhibition on them.

Mankind is now putting to an extreme test God's steadfast love for his creation which Jesus fully demonstrated on the cross. Our rulers have acquired the power to destroy civilisation and damage the environment irreparably, and having acquired it they are losing political and moral control of it. We are edging toward a worldwide crucifixion.

If there were no pilgrimage this Holy Week, we would at best be indicating that the central messages of the Christian faith have nothing to say about the drift towards nuclear war. At worst we would be signalling our acquiescence. We cannot remain silent.

Our pilgrimage is firstly one of repentance, that the Church by the poverty of its witness for peace is partly to blame for the present crisis. Secondly we assert the triumph of life over death and our conviction that 'the cross is mighter than the bomb.' We respond to that conviction by renewing our personal commitment to peacemaking.

Lastly we affirm that the world divided by the arms race into East and West, rich and poor, feared and fearing can by the risen Christ be made one. While the nuclear powers show a scandalous lack of interest in the politics of reconciliation, in trust-building and disarmament, we can do no better than agree with a group of our fellow Christians in Dresden.

In a letter to the head of their East German government they say: 'A readiness to make unilateral confidence building gestures rather than repay like with like is the sole possibility of safeguarding peace today. This belief stems from the message of Jesus Christ.'

Your reaction

1   Explain in your own words why John Gummer criticised the march (paragraph 2).
2   What example is given by the writer to show how Jesus challenged the accepted views of his time? (paragraph 3)
3   Explain what the writer thinks Jesus meant by 'true leadership'. (paragraph 4)
4   Why, according to the writer, do rulers believe in the value of nuclear weapons? (paragraphs 5 and 6)
5   What reasons does the writer give for not agreeing with the possession of nuclear weapons? (paragraphs 6,7,8)
6   What reasons does the writer give for going on the Holy Week pilgrimage? (paragraphs 9,10,11)
7   Write a letter to the *Methodist Recorder* from a Christian who does not agree with the points of view in this article.
8   State and explain your own opinion about:
   (a) the possession of nuclear weapons,
   (b) Christians taking part in marches of this kind at Easter.

Ascension Day

Forty days after Easter Day is Ascension Day. Tradition says that the risen Christ remained with his disciples for 40 days before he was finally taken up into heaven. This final departure from the earth is remembered on Ascension Day.

Credo

He ascended into heaven,
and is seated at the right hand of the Father   (*from the Apostles' Creed*)

Whitsun

Whitsun falls on the seventh Sunday after Easter. It is the festival which celebrates the gift of the Holy Spirit to the Church, and recalls the story in the Acts of the Apostles, Chapter 2.

Credo

I believe in the Holy Spirit   (*from the Apostles' Creed*)

We believe in the Holy Spirit,
the Lord, the giver of life,
who proceeds from the Father (and the Son)
who with the Father (and the Son) together
is worshipped and glorified.
Who spoke through the prophets.

(from the Nicene Creed)

Festivals of Mary

To Orthodox, Roman Catholic and many Anglican Christians, Mary is the first among the saints. She has a very special position in these Churches, because her body was chosen by God to be the bearer of his son. She was the means by which God came to earth in the form of a man by taking a human body. The Roman Catholic Church teaches that Mary must have been herself without sin. If this was so, she must have been born without *original sin* and this is what Roman Catholics mean when they talk of her *Immaculate Conception*. It is common for Catholics to pray to Mary, often as they count off the beads on a rosary.

Roman Catholic and Orthodox tradition also teaches that Mary was a virgin all her life, and that she never had any other children. The Orthodox Church has three special words to describe Mary:

Theotokos Mother of God
Aeiparthenos Ever Virgin
Panagia All-Holy

The festival of the Annunciation is important to Catholics everywhere. This festival is in memory of the visit of the angel Gabriel to Mary (Luke 1:26–38)

The Virgin Hodegetria. The Orthodox Church in particular insists that Mary is honoured, not because of the sort of person she was, but because of her son. By worshipping Mary, the Orthodox reminds himself of the truth that God was made man. Look at the way the Virgin is pointing to the infant Jesus. This is to show that he is the important figure. She is only Holy because of who he is.

The Dormition. The Orthodox Church keeps the feast of the Dormition, and the Catholic Church that of the Assumption. These beliefs state that Mary 'fell asleep' and was the first of redeemed humanity to be received into heaven. In the icon Jesus has come to take Mary's soul.

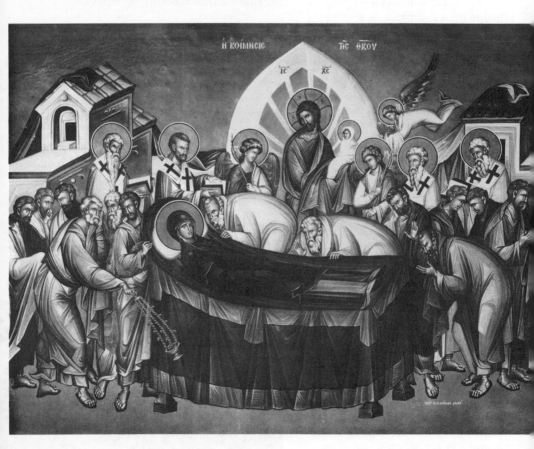

What do you think this man is doing, and why?

Agricultural festivals

Most religions have at some time been closely associated with agriculture, nature and the land. Agricultural festivals were held in Britain before the coming of Christianity, but once Christianity became established there was no difficulty in giving a new meaning to the ancient festivals. The best known of all the agricultural festivals is Harvest, yet oddly enough this is the most recent, only taking its present form in the nineteenth century.

There are four agricultural festivals which are still celebrated in many country areas, and they all have something to say about the Christian concept of God.

Plough Sunday

On Plough Sunday, in February, local farmers bring a plough into Church at the time of ploughing the fields and sowing the seed.

Rogation Sunday

In many country parishes, villagers of all denominations take part in a Rogation Sunday procession around the fields in early spring. In the picture above you can see the parish priest blessing a potato field. This procession is usually well attended – even by people who do not often go to Church.

Lammas

Lammas has been largely forgotten these days, but was in fact the earliest harvest thanksgiving. The name is thought to come from the words 'loaf mass'. It was the day when local farmers and farm workers brought to Church a loaf of bread made from the first wheat to be harvested. When the weather does not permit this (at the beginning of August) farmers present the first harvested sheaves of grain at the offertory during the Eucharist.

Harvest Festival

In rural areas Harvest is one of the greatest celebrations of the year. In a year when the weather has been poor, farmers are only too well aware that their livelihood depends on powers beyond their control, and the relief felt when the crop is finally gathered in is expressed in lusty singing of hymns such as 'Come, ye thankful people, come, / Raise the song of Harvest Home. . . .'

Credo

I believe in God, the Father Almighty, maker of heaven and Earth.

(from the Apostles' Creed)

Suggestions for coursework

1   Find out about
(a) the origins of *and*
(b) the present day practice of
some or all of the four agricultural festivals. (K)
2   What elements of the festival(s) you have chosen demonstrate Christian belief, and what elements come from non-Christian origins? (U)
3   'The Agricultural festivals are nothing but pagan superstition, and have no place in the Christian life.' Give your reasons for agreeing or disagreeing with this statement. (E)
4   Some people say that the traditional Harvest Festival has no meaning for people living in the inner cities. Give your reasons for agreeing or disagreeing with this point of view. If you agree, suggest a form of Harvest thanksgiving which might be more relevant to people living in cities. (E)
5   Write a harvest festival service for use in your school. You should include:
(a) An introductory talk about what Harvest is and what it means. (K/U)
(b) A reading (it need not be from the Bible), and an explanation as to why you have chosen it. (K/U)
(c) A song written by yourself. You may state which tune you wish to be used, or you can write your own. (K/U/E)
(d) A harvest thanksgiving prayer written by yourself. (K/U/E)

Round-up activity: The Festivals Card Game

Making and playing with these cards will help you to remember the names and importance of the major Christian festivals.

How to make the cards
You will need:
 five different colours of card
 coloured pens
 scissors
 (Letter stencils if you have them)

Make a list of all the special days, festivals and seasons in the Christian calendar. Ask your teacher to check the spellings, and to make sure that you have not left any out. Count the list to see how many names you have.

 Cut up each colour card into playing-card-sized pieces. You will need as many pieces of each colour card as you have names on your list.

Using colour A Write (clearly) the name of a special day, festival, or season on each card.
Using colour B Draw a picture or symbol for each festival, etc., each on a different card.
Using colour C For each festival, etc., write a brief account on a card of the event or story celebrated on that day.
Using colour D For each festival, etc., write a brief description on a card of a custom associated with the event.
Using colour E For each festival, etc., write out one verse of a hymn associated with that day, season or festival.

For each of your days / seasons / festivals you should now have five different cards.

How to play

You can use these cards to play a number of games – Happy Families, Snap (two cards belonging to the same festival), or Pairs. The cards will be most helpful in games where you have to collect sets of a type. This will teach you to recognise which customs, beliefs, stories and symbols are connected with each festival.

Resources

Books
T. Shannon, *Christmas and Easter*, Chichester Project (Lutterworth)
G. Read, J. Rudge, R. Howarth, *Westhill Project Bk 3* (Mary Glasgow)
Collinson and Miller, *Celebrations* (Arnold)
Bailey, *Religious Buildings and Festivals* (Schofield & Sims)

Audio-visual aids
Slide centre, S1473 *Palm Sunday and Maundy Thursday*
             S475   *Holy Saturday and Easter Day*
BBC Filmstrip, *Celebrating Easter*
Pictorial Charts, E745 *Christian Festivals*
Videotext, *Aspects of Christianity*

4 Worship and pilgrimage

Objectives for Chapter 4

1   What you should KNOW.
The different forms of public worship, especially the *Eucharist*. The names of the Eucharist, Mass, Holy Communion, etc.
Private prayer; pilgrimage, especially to Rome, Lourdes, the Holy Land and Walsingham.
The Bible and its use in public and private prayer.

2   What you should UNDERSTAND.
(a) *New words and technical terms*
Eucharist; prayer; Bible; ritual; pilgrimage; Church; worship; veneration; adoration; icon; priest; deacon; bishop; iconostasis; lectern; pulpit; altar; liturgy
(b) *People, writings and traditions*
(i) People: Jesus, priests, ministers; lay people.
(ii) Writings: the Bible.
(iii) Traditions: the main difference among Christian traditions in forms of worship.
(c) *Belief*
The Christian beliefs expressed through worship
(d) *Moral issues*
e.g. Should Christians go to church regularly?
(e) *Questions about the meaning of life,*
e.g. What is the value of prayer? What is the value of receiving Communion?

3   What you should be able to DO.
Evaluate on the basis of evidence and argument questions arising from the study of this chapter.

Worship on TV

The first thing you should do before starting on this chapter is to watch two or three acts of worship on television, or listen to them on the radio. At least one service is televised every Sunday on BBC and ITV. Pay careful attention to what is going on, and make a note of any special actions performed by the congregation, the priest or minister, and by any other people performing some special task. Try to spot differences between the services you watch.

Times and places of worship

Word associations

1   Write down any words which come to your mind in connection with the word 'worship'.
2   While you are studying this chapter, collect any pictures which you think have something to do with worship. They may be pictures of people worshipping, or of something which inspires worship. Make a collage of the pictures and words which your class have come up with.

The word 'worship' is connected to the idea of *serving*. Some town officials are called 'Your Worship' or 'The worshipful. . .'. This means that they are considered *worthy* to be served. Sometimes people are inspired to worship by a beautiful natural sight – such as the Victoria Falls in Africa. Worship is often accompanied by feelings of awe, peace, happiness, love, respect, duty, one's own smallness and insignificance; and by the greatness, superiority and wonder of what is worshipped. Sometimes people need to express their feelings outwardly. They might bow down, kneel, raise their hands and faces, cry or shout.

Ask if anyone in your group is prepared to talk about an experience they have had which has led to feelings like these – at a pop concert perhaps, or a sports fixture.

Christian worship

Most Christians, like people of other faiths, worship together regularly.

Sunday

Most Christian communities come together to worship on Sunday. The tradition of having one day in the week which is 'holy' (literally a holy-day) comes from Judaism. The Jews look back to the story in Genesis which says that God created the world in six days and rested on the seventh, and also to the Ten Commandments, one of which says that they shall 'remember the Sabbath Day and keep it holy'. The Jewish Sabbath begins on Friday and ends on Saturday, but the Christian Holy Day is Sunday in memory of the day on which Jesus rose from the dead.

Group activity

Here are four phrases using the word 'Church', but each time the word is used in a different way. Explain what you think the word means in each case.
1 'The Church's one foundation is Jesus Christ our Lord' (first line of a hymn).
2 'Being by God's Ordinance, according to Our just Title, Defender of the Faith, and Supreme Governor of the Church, within these Our Dominions. . .' (His Majesty's Declaration, Preface to the 39 Articles of Belief, Church of England).
3 'We ask that we your church, may shine as a light in this community, that all our friends and neighbours may come to love and worship you also' (prayer).
4 'On Sunday, we open the appeal for the restoration of the Church roof' (parish magazine).

The Church building

In the past when everyone was a Christian in name at least, so many people attended worship that large buildings were needed to hold them all. This is why in many towns and villages the church is still the largest building. Modern churches tend to be smaller because they were built to hold fewer people. It is not actually necessary for Christians to meet for worship in a church, and as we shall see, many meet in each other's houses on a regular basis.

However, the majority of Christians all over the world still worship in special buildings which may be called churches or chapels, or meeting houses. Some very large churches are called *cathedrals*, and they are normally Roman Catholic, Anglican or Orthodox. The cathedral is where the bishop has his seat, and is the centre of a *diocese* or administrative area which he governs.

Your school will be in an Anglican, a Roman Catholic and an Orthodox Diocese. See if you can find out the names of all three, and the names of all three Bishops.

Group activity

How many places of worship (Christian) can you spot on your journey to and from school, or near where you live? Make a note of as many as you can, noting their NAME, what they look like, any particular features which catch your attention (e.g. posters, statues, special windows).

Select *two* of these buildings and make a careful study of any notice-boards which may be outside the building, fastened to the wall, or in the porch. Make a note of any information which you think might be important in helping you to understand what goes on in the building, or how it is run. You might look for the following:
Times and days of services . . . number of Sunday services . . . who is in charge – does he/she have a special title, such as Rector or Minister?

... what other activities go on apart from worship? ... when is the building open? ... what denomination is it?

You may be able to get a copy of a magazine which will tell you even more about the place.

Next lesson, talk about what the whole class has discovered. What conclusions can you draw, and what can you learn from the class researches? You could make a wall display about 'Churches near our School'.

Summary

Make a summary of what you have discovered so far about churches just by looking at the outside of buildings. You should include the following headings and add any others which you think are important.
1   Names of buildings
2   Titles of people in responsible positions
3   Names of services
4   Numbers of services
5   Other activities apart from worship which may take place
6   Names of the denominations in the area
7   Style of the building

Talking pictures

So far, we have only talked about what we can discover about the activity of the Church from the outside of buildings. This may tell us a lot about when Christians worship, but little about *why* they do it, or what it means to them.

First thoughts

Here are three pictures of Christians at worship. Look at them carefully and discuss the following questions with a friend or partner.
1   How would you describe:
(a) What the people in the pictures are doing with their *eyes*?
(b) What the people in the pictures are doing with their *hands*?
(c) What the people in the pictures are doing with their *arms*?
2   Choose eight people in the pictures. Look carefully at each of these people and in each case write down any words which you feel describe their expression, or how you think they are feeling.

Talking from experience

Have you ever attended an act of Christian worship? If so, talk to your partner about it. (If you have attended more than one, choose one which sticks in your mind.) What do you remember about it? What was the occasion – was it a regular Sunday service or something special, a wedding perhaps? What did you like/dislike about it? Did you notice anything special about other people there? Who was leading the service (if anyone)? Where did it take place? What were the surroundings like? Was it formal or informal? Was anyone wearing special clothes?

Bring together the memories of the whole class and make a class summary of 'experiences of Christian worship'. You might also discuss why some people feel quite positively about acts of worship they have attended whereas others have very negative feelings. Is it just a matter of how 'lively' or 'atmospheric' the service was?

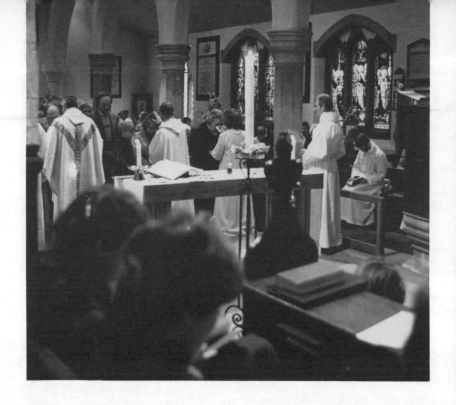

Styles of worship

If you were to walk into two services one Sunday, one in a Baptist church and another in, say, an Anglican church, certain differences would strike you immediately.

The Protestant tradition

Many Protestant and some Anglican communities prefer a simple service, with little ceremony, few decorations, and a great emphasis on the Bible and its teachings. The altar, more likely called the Communion Table, may be the focal point, and on it may be a vase of flowers and/or a Bible. There may be a cross, but not always. The Minister or Pastor may wear a black gown, and sometimes a white surplice, but no elaborate vestments. (Special robes are worn in Catholic, Orthodox and Anglican churches.) If the service is a celebration of Holy Communion, it will follow a set pattern. Other services will often not be planned in detail, but will consist of prayers, Bible readings, preaching and singing. Prayer may be *extempore* which means a person will pray what comes into their mind at the time, although traditional prayers such as the Lord's Prayer are also used. The people are often free to express themselves when and how they choose. Some people may clap their hands, others may call out 'Yes, Lord' or 'Hallelujah' when someone else says something they agree with. Some Churches are *Charismatic* – this includes some Anglican and Roman Catholic communities. This means that people in the congregation have received the 'baptism of the Spirit' which gives them the gift of *tongues*. 'Speaking in tongues' was a common practice in the early Church.

Most people recognise the Salvation Army. Salvationists hold regular outdoor services which anyone can attend. It is a way of showing their faith to everyone, and it gives all sorts of people an opportunity to join in worship without having to go into a church.

The Society of Friends

One of the simplest forms of congregational worship is that of the Society of Friends (Quakers). The Friends meet in a plain building, with no decoration, no priest or minister, and nothing to use but a Bible and other books which are available if someone wishes to use one. People arrive and sit in silence. This may continue for an hour unless someone is inspired to say something. If one person speaks, another may respond to what they have said, but no one is under any pressure to say anything. Quakers believe that every person can establish his or her own relationship with God, and can communicate with him, without the need for priests or ministers.

Liturgical worship

Worship in Roman Catholic, Orthodox and Anglican Churches usually follows a written order of service called a *liturgy*. Worship will sometimes be very elaborate, using drama, beautiful music, colourful vestments, candles, bells and incense. The focal point in the church will be the altar, because the sacrifice or offering made at the Eucharist is the most important ritual that takes place. The service will follow a set pattern of words, with some prayers being written for each particular week. Even the Bible readings are laid out for each day of the year so that the whole book is read over a certain period – often two or three years.

The Eucharist

Most Christians recognise the Eucharist as the most important act of public worship. This service has many names:

Eucharist from a Greek verb meaning 'to give thanks'. This is a term which most Christians will be prepared to use. It emphasises the thanks due to God for the gift of his son.

Holy Communion – This term emphasises the sharing nature of the ritual – of everyone coming together to share in the bread and wine. This term is used in some Anglican Churches and a number of Protestant Churches.

Mass – The term used by Roman Catholics. It is thought that the word comes from the word *missa*, which was one of the last words of the Latin Mass. It simply means 'sent out'. However, the central belief about the Mass is that it is a re-enactment of the sacrifice of Jesus on the cross, and that the bread and wine actually become his body and blood.

The Lord's Supper Saint Paul first used this expression. It puts the emphasis on the sharing of a meal in remembrance of Jesus until he comes again. It is a term used by Protestant and some Anglican Churches.

The Breaking of Bread This expression can be found in the Acts of the Apostles. It is another Protestant expression, again emphasising the sharing and fellowship of a meal.

It may seem at first as though the Churches celebrate completely different rituals. It is true that the names given to the service, and the beliefs that lie behind them, are very different. Also whereas some Churches celebrate the Eucharist every day, others only celebrate once a month, or even twice a year! However, the structure of the service, whether in an Orthodox or Baptist Church, is fundamentally the same. There are four sections in the service, and you would be likely to recognise them in any church you attended.

Preparation – This is sometimes called the ministry of the word, and is the part of the service where confession of sins is made, prayers are said, the Bible read, a sermon preached and perhaps a collection taken. It will end with the bread and wine being put on the altar or table.

The Consecration – This is the most solemn part of the service. The crucial point is where the priest or celebrant repeats the words spoken by Jesus at the Last Supper (Mark 14:22–25).

Communion – The celebrant and the people share in the bread and wine.

Dismissal – There is a final thanksgiving and usually a blessing. There may be a prayer encouraging everyone to go into the world and make sure that the service they have attended makes some practical difference to their lives.

The Eucharist in the Western Church

Because the Eucharist follows a set form of words, it is written down in prayer books. In the Roman Catholic Church this book is called the *MISSAL*; in the Church of England it is the *ALTERNATIVE SERVICE BOOK*.

One important difference is that the Protestant Churches have ministers whereas the other two have priests.

1   As people arrive, they usually kneel or sit to pray quietly for a moment and prepare themselves for the service.

2   Meanwhile, in the **vestry** the Priest or Minister will be preparing for the service. All Roman Catholic and most Anglican priests wear **vestments**, traditional clothes which date back many centuries. They are not necessary for the service to take place but are part of the tradition of the Churches. To the left of the priest you can see the **chalice** with the **paten** resting on top of it and a cover draped over the two. The Priest will carry them into the church and put them on the altar.

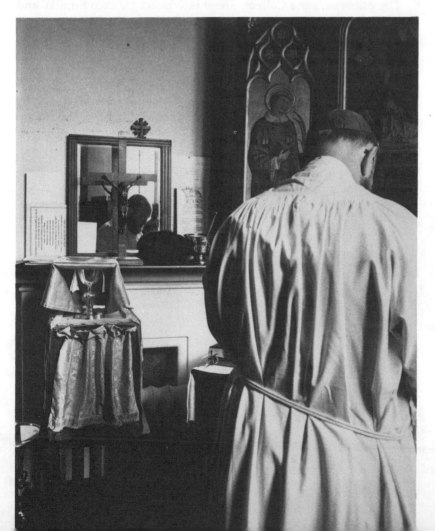

The preparation

3   When the priest or minister enters, the congregation stand, and usually a hymn will be sung. In Roman Catholic and Anglican churches, the priest often has helpers called servers or acolytes who may be carrying candles or incense if it is used.

Children are welcomed at all Church services, but are likely to become bored. They are usually taken out at the beginning of the service for their own study group. They come back before the Communion.

4   The service begins with a prayer of **confession** when the congregation say that they are sorry for any sins they have committed. The priest then gives the **absolution** or forgiveness. In the Anglican rite this comes later, after the Intercession.

5   The service continues with the singing of the **Gloria**, an ancient hymn which begins with the words 'Glory be to God on High, and on Earth peace, good will toward men'. Where have you heard these words before?

6   The priest says the **Collect**. There is a collect for each Sunday and for special days such as festivals and saints' days. A collect is a prayer which draws the attention of the congregation to the main theme for the day.

7   Next come the Bible readings. There may be an Old Testament reading, and there will certainly be a reading from one of the New Testament books *apart from* the Gospels. These two are often read by a member of the congregation who will normally stand at the lectern to read.

Reading from the lectern – the annual clowns' service at St James's Church, Piccadilly.

The priest or deacon reads the **Gospel** for the day. The Gospel may be carried to the middle of the church for this reading. Everyone stands and faces the Gospel, and in some churches incense is waved over the Gospel, and the priest makes the sign of the cross (as above).
8   The priest or deacon delivers his **sermon** from the **pulpit**. He or she will usually base the sermon on the theme of the Bible readings. The Congregation sits to listen.
9   Everyone stands for the saying of the **Nicene Creed**.
10   The people sit or kneel for the **Intercessions**. These are prayers asking for God's (and sometimes for the Saints') help and guidance. Prayers may be said for (among other things); the Church; the nations of the world; the Queen and those in authority; the local community; family; friends; the sick; those who have died. These prayers are often led by a member of the congregation.

The consecration

1   In the Anglican Church everyone exchanges the **peace**. The priest turns to the congregation and says, 'The Peace of the Lord be always with you', and they reply 'And also with you'. Families and friends may exchange a kiss or a hug, or just shake hands, saying to one another 'Peace be with you'. In the Roman Catholic Mass this comes later in the service.

2   The Offertory. The bread and wine is taken to the altar and given to the priest. If there is a collection, it is taken at this point while a hymn is sung, and the money is also offered along with the bread and wine. The priest puts the bread on the paten and the wine in the **chalice**. Some Protestant and a few Anglican Churches do not use wine, but use grape juice instead. Also they may use individual small glasses instead of one cup.

Two Indian girls bring the bread and wine to the altar.

3   The **Eucharistic Prayer**. There are a number of different forms of this prayer, all dating back to ancient times. There are three parts to the prayer:

   (a) Thanksgiving – for the salvation of humanity
   (b) The Sanctus which is sung by the choir or everyone.
      Holy, holy, holy
      Lord God of Hosts,
      Heaven and Earth are full of thy glory.
      Glory be to thee, O Lord.

> ### Research
> (i) Find out where the words of the Sanctus come from.
> (ii) Why do you think these words came to be included in the Eucharist at this point?

   (c) the '**Proper Preface**' or **consecration**.

The consecration during High Mass at Westminster Cathedral.

The priest or minister asks that the bread and wine will become for the worshippers the body and blood of Christ. He repeats the words spoken by Jesus at the Last Supper.

The Roman Catholic Church teaches the doctrine of **transubstantiation**. This is the belief that the bread and wine actually become the body and blood of Jesus, even though they do not look any different. A bell may be rung at this, the most solemn part of the service. In the Roman Catholic Church prayers are said at this point for the Pope, bishops and priests.

4   Everyone joins in the Lord's Prayer. At this point in the Roman Catholic Church, the peace is exchanged.

5   The choir or the congregation sing or say the **Agnus Dei** while the priest breaks the bread.

> *O Lamb of God, you take away the sins of the world, have mercy upon us;*
> *O Lamb of God, you take away the sins of the world, have mercy upon us;*
> *O Lamb of God, you take away the sins of the world. Grant us thy peace.*

'This is my body which was given for you. Do this in remembrance of me.'
'This is my blood of the New Covenant. Do this as often as you drink it in remembrance of me.'

In the Methodist Church the bread is handed to people on a plate and they take their own. This sometimes happens in Anglican churches. In some Churches there is a custom that each person gives a piece of bread to the next.

The Communion
6   In an Anglican Church most people kneel at the altar rail. They are given first the bread and then the wine.

7   Members of the congregation return to their seat for a few moments of quiet prayer.

The dismissal
8   The service ends with the blessing from the priest or minister.

Roman Catholics receive the body and blood of Christ. This is received standing.

Check your reading

Here are some important words which you have met so far in this chapter, but the letters of each word have been muddled up. See how quickly you can discover each one, and write a few words to show that you understand its importance in Christian worship.

SSDMISLAI   ESRECIV   CRSACITIHAM   EBLIB
RATAL   RMNSEO   EPECA   PLGSOE   AEBLT
SSAM   TPPIUL   NATEP   TPERIS   TYLIA
CHCHRU   YIRGUTL   STSTMVEEN   PROWIHS
LRTUAI   YSTREV   CRTEENL   SSCNIOEFON
CCLLOET   DEREC   FTFOORREY   CAIELHC
TACERSIHU   ITRESOSNECSIN

The Orthodox liturgy

The Eucharist, otherwise known as the Divine Liturgy, is the most important service in the Orthodox Church. The service follows a pattern which dates back to the fourth century AD and possibly earlier. The setting is very elaborate. Most Orthodox churches have paintings all over the walls, and the priests and servers leading the worship will be dressed in colourful vestments, often embroidered in gold. Incense is used throughout the service, which is chanted, led by a choir. But most spectacular of all are the icons. The Church is divided in two by the *iconostasis* or 'icon screen' which you can see in the picture below. This is a wooden screen painted with icons.

The Iconostasis and Royal Doors in the Church of the Community of St John the Baptist at Tolleshunt Knights in Essex. The icons were all painted by one of the sisters in the monastery.

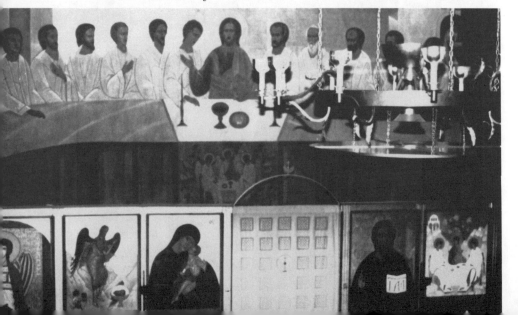

This woman is Russian and she has just arrived at her church in Moscow for the Sunday Eucharist. Like everyone else who comes, she will have bought a candle and lit it, placing it in a special holder. Now she has gone to the front of the church where she crosses herself and kisses the icon. She will now join the other women who are standing at one side of the church, while the men stand on the other. There are no seats, although some elderly people bring folding stools for when they get tired. Meanwhile, the priest is preparing the bread and wine in the chapel of preparation.

There is a double door in the centre called the 'ROYAL DOOR'. In the *sanctuary* behind the screen is the altar or *Holy Table*.

The preparation
The service begins with the **Litany of Peace**. The priest says short prayers and the people respond with the words *Kyrie Eleison* which mean 'Lord have Mercy'. This is followed by the singing of a **Psalm**, after which comes the **Little Litany**, the people again responding *Kyrie Eleison*. Then the **Beatitudes** (see p.148) are read. Then comes the **Little Entrance**, when the priest and servers process carrying the Gospels high above their heads so that everyone can see them. The choir and people sing the **Trisagion** at least three times.

Holy God, holy and mighty, holy and immortal, have mercy upon us.

Then follows the climax of this part of the service, the Bible readings from the Psalms, the Epistles and the Gospels. The Priest then delivers his **sermon** and the first section of the Liturgy ends with prayers.

The Consecration
This, the second part of the Liturgy, begins with the **Great Entrance**, a magnificent procession of servers bringing candles and incense, and the priests bringing the bread and wine. The people bow as they

The Priest at the Holy Table – an Orthodox cathedral in London.

pass, and the Royal Doors are opened, allowing the priest to pass through to the sanctuary and lay the bread and wine upon the **Holy Table**.

The congregration greet each other with the **kiss of peace** and say the **Nicene Creed**. The priest says the **Eucharistic Prayers** which include the story of the last supper, after which everyone joins in the **Lord's Prayer**.

As the Liturgy reaches its climax, the priest raises the bread and breaks it. This is called **Elevation** and **Fraction**. While he is doing this, the choir sings, and bells are rung. Then comes the climax of the whole service.

The Communion
The priest stands before the Royal Doors and the people receive bread dipped in wine, served on a spoon.

The Dismissal
There follow the Thanksgiving and the blessing.

Symbols and art
As we have seen, Churches vary tremendously in their use of colour, ritual and ceremony. Not surprisingly, it is the Roman Catholic, Orthodox and Anglican Churches which have most use for elaborate artwork and ritual objects. But many Anglican and Catholic Churches look quite plain – there are great variations even within one tradition.

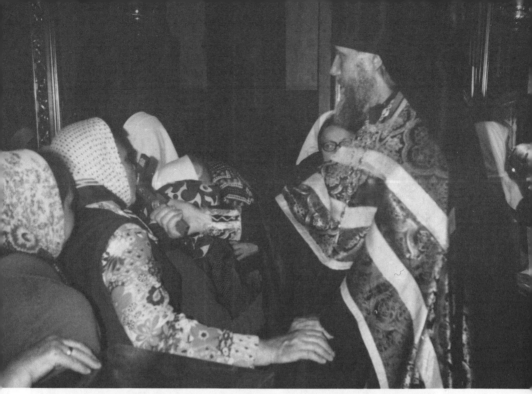

When the Liturgy is over, there is a final ceremony when the congregation come forward and kiss the cross. Everyone receives a small piece of bread called the **Antidoron** *as a sign of sharing, and in memory of the* **agape**, *the meal which the early Christians used to share together.*

But the paintings, wall hangings, stained glass windows, gold and silver which can be found in these churches are not just there for decoration. If you look at them closely, you will find that they all contain within their design something which tells you about the Christian faith. You may look at a beautiful window which tells the story of the creation, or you may find a set of richly-embroidered vestments or kneelers which have been decorated with Christian symbols, full of meaning. Many Christians, as we have seen, dislike the presence of ritual objects in Church. They say that they are a distraction from prayer. Others point to the vast wealth of some Churches contained in their treasures, and say that this should be sold and the money given to the poor. Some say that the use of statues and icons in Catholic and Orthodox churches comes close to idolatry, and if you visit some of the older churches and Cathedrals in Europe, you will often find that the heads of statues, brasses and paintings have been destroyed. This was done during the *Reformation* by Protestants who believed that the presence of these human likenesses gave rise to idol worship. Others find that contemplating things of great beauty which incorporate symbols of the Christian faith helps them concentrate on prayer. The use of ritual objects in worship is largely a matter of personal taste.

Group activity

Here are some pictures of items you might find in a church. Below, in Box A are the names of the items in the pictures. They are not in the same order as the pictures. Ignore the asterisks for now.
In Box B are the descriptions of the objects in the pictures. They are in a different order still.

Your job is to match the correct name and description with each picture. You could work in groups of two or three.

Box A

1   Cross
2   Crucifix *
3   Mother and child
4   Monstrance
5   Crozier
6   Candles
7   Tapestry *
8   Frontal *
9   Lectern covers *
10 Stole *
11 Chasuble *
12 Sanctuary lamp
13 Thurible and boat
14 Chalice
15 Paten

a   b   c

d

e

f

g

h

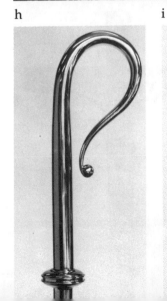

i

j

k

l

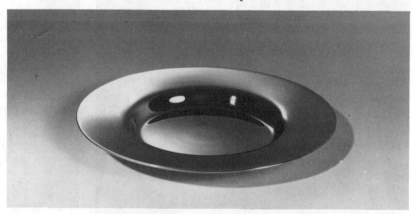

m

n

o

Box B

This is now part of a priest or deacon's vestments. It was part of ancient Roman costume. Worn by a deacon over one shoulder and tied under the opposite arm. Worn by a priest over both shoulders like a scarf.

Usually made of metal – often gold or silver. It has a glass disc built in through which can be seen a 'host' – a communion wafer which has been blessed. Often kept in a special chapel in Catholic churches and sometimes used to bless the congregation. When it is held up, the congregation might bow to the ground.

The most common symbol of the Christian faith. Most churches have one on the altar or in another prominent place. Many people wear a small gold one on a chain around their neck.

Found mainly in Catholic churches but also some Anglican. A reminder of the first among the Saints and the incarnation which gave her her importance.

Very common in churches of most denominations. Once used for practical purposes in the days before electricity, etc. Now preserved for symbolic significance. A very special one, highly decorated, is used at Easter and at Baptisms, in memory of Jesus saying 'I am the light of the world'.

Made largely for decoration. The importance lies in the design. The largest one in the world is in Coventry Cathedral.

With the figure, a constant reminder that Jesus died for the sins of the world. More common in Catholic than Protestant churches.

Derived from a standard garment worn in the later days of the Roman Empire. Part of a priest or bishop's vestments – worn over the stole.

Used to carry and to burn incense. The incense is spooned out of one container and into the other, where a charcoal fire has been lit. It will then be carried by a server/acolyte who swings it gently so that the smoke fills the Church. It may be waved over the congregation and over the Bible.

In Roman Catholic and some Anglican churches this hangs above the altar. Tradition says that it is probably in memory of the lamp that burnt always in the Temple in Jerusalem. Something very similar may be found in synagogues.

Mainly decorative, but the design is the important thing. Most Churches that use vestments will use these, and the colour and design may match the sets of vestments. Because they are hanging in a prominent position, their colour reminds the congregation of the season.

Carried by a bishop. Being shaped in the style of a shepherd's crook, it reminds him that he is the representative of Christ on earth. Just as Jesus called himself the 'good shepherd' so he must care for his 'flock'.

Used to cover the front of an altar. Like vestments, the colour will often change with the season or festival.

Symbols

Look at the photographs again. Those marked with asterisks in the list on p. 112 carry designs in the form of important symbols. Here are the names and descriptions of the symbols. See how quickly you can match the names and descriptions to the right symbols. (NB Some pictures carry more than one symbol.)

The Good Shepherd. This is in memory of Jesus saying 'I am the good shepherd'. This was one of the earliest representations of Jesus, and 'good shepherd' drawings have been found in the catacombs at Rome dating back to the second century.

The Chi Rho. A very ancient Christian symbol, also found in the catacombs. These are the first two letters of the Greek word for Christ – Χρ.

The loaves and fishes. This is a very popular symbol for the Eucharist. It commemorates the time when Jesus fed the five thousand. In St John's gospel especially, this story is seen as a symbol for the Eucharist, and afterwards Jesus said. 'I am the bread of life. Anyone who eats this bread will never die'. The sign of the fish has had a special importance for Christians from the earliest days. The Greek word for fish is *ichthus*. The letters of the word in Greek are the first letters of the words:

Iesus – Jesus
Christos – Christ
Theos – God
'Uios – Son
Soter – Saviour

The dove is the symbol of peace, but is also the symbol of the Holy Spirit. It is usually featured on red vestments, frontals, etc., which are used at Whitsun, the festival of the Holy Spirit.

Fire is also usually represented with the dove to remind worshippers of the baptism of the Spirit received by the disciples in the Upper Room, which enabled them to speak in tongues.

Wheat is a symbol of life. It also reminds Christians of the bread which they take at the Eucharist, and of the time when Jesus said, 'I am the bread of life'.

INRI These letters are often shown above a crucifix. They stand for the words which Pontius Pilate is said to have had written above the cross:

Jesus of Nazareth, King (*rex*) of the Jews.

The vine is another popular Eucharistic symbol. Jesus said 'I am the vine', and it is the vine which **gives** the wine which is consecrated to become the body and blood of Christ.

Alpha Omega. In the book of Revelation, Jesus says, I am the Alpha and the Omega, the beginning and the end. Alpha (A) is the first letter of the Greek alphabet and Omega (Ω) is the last. This symbol symbolises that Christ is timeless, eternal – existing from all time and to all eternity – without beginning and without end.

Symbols game
To help you learn the symbols and their meaning, you could adapt the Festivals Card Game on p. 91. This time you will need three colour cards – one for the symbol, one for its name and one for the meaning. See how many more Christian symbols you can find for your game.

Display work
Make two collages of pictures and words:
1 Things to look for in a church;
2 Christian symbols and their meanings.

Coursework – Why do people go to church? A survey
Some schools may feel that it is not possible to do this activity because it will need considerable preparation. However, if you do try it, it could form the basis of a piece of coursework, or it could simply be used to increase your understanding of other people, what things are important to them, and what they believe. You will need the cooperation of the churches you work with. *Under no circumstances* should this activity be prepared without their agreement. Once you have got this agreement and have prepared your questionnaires, the bulk of the fieldwork can be done on one Sunday and the follow-up work in two or three lessons at school.

The task
Conduct a survey over as many local churches as possible. *Find out* why people go to certain churches and not others (e.g. the denomination, they like the vicar, atmosphere, building, people); what they like and don't like about different styles of worship (e.g. music, ceremony, simplicity, quiet/noise); why they go to Church at all (e.g. to communicate with God, meet people); the average attendance at each service (the priest/minister can tell you this from the records); why the congregation think that attendance is high or low.

The class will have to divide into as many groups as there are churches to be surveyed. Bring together your results and analyse them. What conclusions can you draw? Remember to let the churches concerned have copies of your findings – they will probably be very interested!

Suggestions for coursework

1 SYMBOLS
Knowledge
Either
(i) Select a suitable number (depending on what syllabus you are studying) of the first seven pictures on pp. 112–13. Name and describe each object, giving an account of its use in Christian worship. Do *not* copy the descriptions in this book, but use your own words and try to find out more information from a library, churches, or manufacturers.
or
(ii) Design either a set of vestments and lectern/pulpit covers for use at the Eucharist during a named season of the Church's year; or a tapestry; or a set of six kneelers.
Your design must include suitable symbols and should be in colour. Write a description of the items you have designed saying what they are called, how they are used and the names of any symbols you have included.

Understanding
Explain carefully why the following symbols are often used as decoration on objects used during the Eucharist.
(a) Loaves and fishes
(b) The vine
(c) The cross, or a crucifix.

Evaluation
'It's about time the Church stopped buying expensive vestments, gold and silver-plated chalices and the like. If they sold the lot they would make millions of pounds which could be given to the poor.' What answers might be given to this statement by (a) a Christian who agreed with it and (b) by a Christian who did not agree with it? What is your own view?

2 COMPARING ACTS OF WORSHIP
Knowledge
Write a description of a Eucharistic service which you have (preferably) attended, or have seen on television. Make sure that you state the denomination.

Understanding
Compare the service you attended with that of another denomination. Make a list of similarities and differences, and explain carefully why there are differences in both belief and practice between the two.

Evaluation

Either

The use of vestments, bells, incense, ritual, music and ceremony can arouse very strong feelings between Christians even today. Some love it; some hate it; and others think it is unchristian. Why do you think these issues are so important to some Christians? How important do *you* think they are?

Or

'I am a Christian, but I don't go to church. It doesn't do anything for me at all.' How important do you think Church attendance should be for people who call themselves Christians?

3 SOLVING A PROBLEM

The Architect

Here is a ground plan showing what remains of a church which burnt down in 1985.

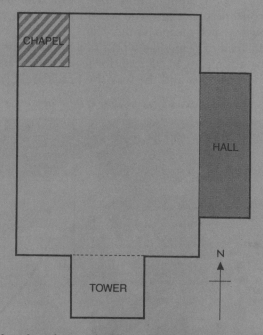

In 1985, the church was burnt to the ground. All that remained were the four walls, and a sixteenth-century chapel.

The Vicar has launched a competition for young people in the Parish to enter plans for the rebuilding of the inside of the church. You are about to design your entry.

The only instructions you have are as follows:

1 There are to be two areas for worship – one to hold about 100 people, and the other to hold about 12 people.

2   There are to be two meeting rooms, one large and one small.
3   The building is to be used for concerts and plays during the week.
4   The insurance money from the fire was not enough to pay for the rebuilding. Luckily, the Baptist congregation, whose church is on the verge of collapse, have agreed to share the cost if they can share the use of the building.
5   You are to enter designs for two special features in the new church. One of these must be an item of furniture, and the other must be an item of decoration or clothing.

When you have completed the task, write a careful account of how you reached your decisions regarding planning and design.

Icons

It is very unlikely that you could ever find an Orthodox church without icons, and most Orthodox homes have at least one. Icons are more than religious paintings. The word for someone who paints an icon is an 'iconographer', and this word tells us something important about the paintings. The second part of the word is from the Greek *grapho* which means 'write'. Icons are said to be *written* not painted. So instead of being like works of art which are meant to be *looked at* icons are meant to be *read*, for icons have a message (e.g. the halo, hand positions and the way the heads are facing all mean

A workshop in an Orthodox monastery where one of the sisters writes icons.

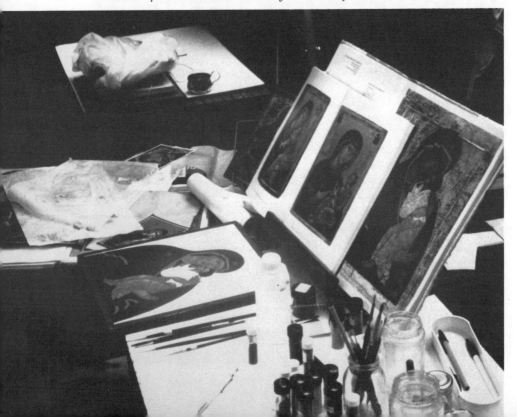

something special). The icon writer is no ordinary painter, and has to have special training, not only in artistic technique, but in spiritual preparation for the work. Before beginning to write an icon, the iconographer has to undergo a period of prayer and fasting, must attend confession and receive the Eucharist.

You have already seen some icons in this book (pp. 88, 108, 109). Some icons tell a story: they might for instance tell the story of Jesus entering Jerusalem. Others are paintings of people – Jesus and Mary being the most popular, then the Saints.

Icons date back to the middle of the fifth century, but in AD 730 they were banned because some people believed that the Moslem defeat of the Christian Empire was a punishment from God because of their worshipping idols, which is how some people saw the icons. But in AD 843 icons were restored to the churches, and since then they have played an important part in Orthodox worship.

An icon is not just a painting on wood; the word also applies to the paintings which decorate Orthodox Churches, often from the floor to the roof. (See p. 108.) An icon is blessed by the priest in church, making it a *holy* icon. From that time the icon may be *venerated*. To venerate something is not to worship it but to *honour* it. Both in the Church and at home, the Orthodox Christians say their prayers before icons, make confession before icons, light candles and burn incense before icons. The icon helps the worshipper in five important ways.

1 The icon is called a 'door'. By passing through this 'door' the worshipper comes face to face with Christ.
2 The icon is a teaching aid. Those which tell a story remind the worshipper of important events in the lives of Christ and the Saints.
3 Icons are important in that they remind the worshipper of the reality of the incarnation. It would be quite wrong to represent God who is invisible in paint, but because he 'became flesh' in Jesus Christ, Jesus may be represented as a reminder that God took human form.
4 Icons are a reminder that the material world, which some Christians have despised, can be a way of expressing the spiritual. The icon is made of wood, but carries a spiritual message.
5 Icons have something to say about being human – that humanity was made in the image of God. God creates, and in imitation of Him, people also are creative, making things of beauty from the raw materials which God has given them.

Coursework on icons
YOU WILL NEED a collection of icons, available as postcards from many art galleries and religious bookshops. Also remember to ask friends who go on holiday in Greece or Russia especially to find postcards for you.

Knowledge
Write a talk for your class, or for assembly, about
(a) how icons are made and/or
(b) what subjects are most commonly shown on icons, and/or
(c) how icons are used in worship.

Understanding
Explain why icons are important for Orthodox Christians and/or
Explain carefully the arguments for and against the use of icons and
how they affected the Orthodox Church in the eighth century.

Evaluation
'Thou shalt not make any graven image . . . thou shalt not bow down
and worship them'. Should these commandments apply to icons?

The Bible in Christian worship

You have already read something in this chapter about the use of the
Bible in worship.

Revision

1   Where would you be likely to find a Bible in
(a) a Protestant church
(b) an Anglican Church
(c) an Orthodox Church?
2   During the Eucharist, what books of the Bible are *likely* to be read,
and what book(s) of the Bible are *always* read?

Lectionaries
A Lectionary is a book, or a table in the back of a prayer book, which
sets out the passages of the Bible to be read every day of the year.

Table 1   Psalms and readings for morning and evening prayer Sundays and
weekdays, year 1

*The first page of the table of readings for the Anglican Church. The readings are
spread over a two-year cycle, so that most of the Bible is read over that period.
Readings are given for each day of the week (SMTWTFS), both for morning and
evening.   (ME)*

		Psalms	First Reading	Second Reading
NINTH SUNDAY BEFORE CHRISTMAS				
(Fifth Sunday before Advent) Green				
S	M	104 or 104.1–25	Prov 8.1, 22–31	Rev 21.1–7, 22–end
	E	148, 150	Gen 2.4b–end	John 3.1–12
M	M	1, 2	Dan 1	Matt 1.18–end
	E	3, 4	Prov 1.1–19 or	
			Ecclus 1.1–10	Rev 1

T	M	5, 6	Dan 2.1–24	Matt 2.1–12
	E	7	Prov 1.20–end or	
			Ecclus 1.11–end	Rev 2.1–11
W	M	8, 9	Dan 2.25–end	Matt 2.13–end
	E	10	Prov 2 or	
			Ecclus 2	Rev 2.12–end
Th	M	11, 12	Dan 3 1–18	Matt 3
	E	13, 14	Prov 3.1–26 or	
			Ecclus 4.11–28	Rev 3.1–13
F	M	15, 16	Dan 3.19–end	Matt 4.1–11
	E	17	Prov 3.27–4.19 or	
			Ecclus 6.14–31	Rev 3.14–end
S	M	18.1–32	Dan 4.1–18	Matt 4.12–22
	E	18.33–end	Prov 6.1–19 or	
			Ecclus 7.27–end	Rev 4

Table 2 There are also special readings for saints' days

	Psalms	First Reading	Second Reading
ST PETER THE APOSTLE (29 June) Red			
M	71	Ezek 2.1–7	Acts 9.32–end
E	145	Ezek 34.11–16	John 21.15–22
If St Paul is commemorated with St Peter the following may be used:			
M	19	Jer 1.4–10	Acts 12.1–11
E	139	Ezek 3.22–end	John 21.15–22
ST THOMAS THE APOSTLE (3 July) Red			
M	34	Job 42.1–6	1 Pet 1.3–9
E	92	2 Sam 15.17–21	John 11.1–16
ST MARY MAGDALEN (22 July) White			
M	32	1 Sam 16.14–end	Luke 8.1–3
E	63	Hosea 14	Mark 15.40–16.8

Group activity

Look at the table for the first week of the first year. (Table 1)
1   How many weeks is it until Christmas?
2   How many weeks is it until Advent begins?
3   What colour vestments etc. will be worn?
4   What will be the Old Testament reading on Wednesday morning?
5   What will be the Psalm on Sunday afternoon?
6   What will be the New Testament reading on Saturday morning?
7   What will be the New Testament reading on Thursday afternoon?

Look at the table of Saints' days (Table 2)
1   What will be the readings for the morning of the feast of St Peter?
Look up the passages and say why they have been chosen for this day.
2   What colour will be worn, and why?
3   What is the date of St Peter's day?

Respect for the Bible
Look back over this chapter, and write down all the actions which show that the Bible, or parts of the Bible, are treated in a special way. You should find seven or eight examples of how the Bible is treated.

Taking each one in turn, explain what the action suggests about the feelings of the person or people involved towards the Bible.

Revision exercise
Just a Minute!
This activity is based on the radio panel game *Just a Minute*.
You will need. . .
1   A stop watch.
2   As many bells, whistles, hooters (anything that makes a noise!) as there are teams.
3   Various artefacts and photographs connected with the Eucharist, e.g. a chalice, paten, items of vestments, Bible, prayer book, missal, crucifix, communion wafers, a loaf of bread, tray of communion glasses, communion wine bottle. Photographs of important things in a church, or of people celebrating the Eucharist at various stages and in different traditions. (You might use some of the pictures in this book.)

The Game
Hide all the objects and put a timekeeper in charge of them and also of the stop watch. (Your teacher would be a good candidate for this job!)
    Divide into teams of four. The timekeeper brings out one of the objects, gives it to the first team and starts the watch. The first person in the first team then has a minute to talk about the object or photograph (you could even have a slide in a slide-viewer).

Rules
Members of the other teams keep their hands on their 'buzzers'. A member of another team may 'buzz' whenever they think that the speaker has done any of the following things:
(a) Repeated something already said
(b) Said something that is inaccurate
(c) Got off the point
(d) Hesitated for more than three seconds.
    The timekeeper will say whether the challenge was valid or not. (The timekeeper's word is final!) If the challenge was valid, the challenger takes over the subject, and gets one point for his/her team. The game continues in this fashion until the minute is up. The person still talking when the time is up gets two points for his/her team.

Pilgrimage and prayer

Pilgrimage
A pilgrimage is a religious journey to a place that has particular importance for people of faith. Pilgrimage is not so important for most Christians as it is to Muslims and Hindus, for example, but, for

some Christians, going on a pilgrimage is an experience which is remembered for a lifetime.

Pilgrimage to the Holy Land
(From an interview with Thomas, aged 20)

Thomas, you spent about £600 on a trip to Israel last Easter. That was a lot of money. Why did you do it?
Thomas   I was converted to Christianity two years ago, and became a member of the Church of England. Someone in our diocese organised a youth pilgrimage to the Holy Land, and since I could just afford it, I thought I'd go. You read so many stories from the Bible about events which happened in Israel, but I suppose for me the most important thing was to go to the places where Jesus lived and worked and died – Bethlehem where he was born, Nazareth where he spent much of his youth, Galilee where he taught and called his disciples, and, of course, Jerusalem where he died and rose again.

Was it just a holiday, or did you hope to get something more out of the visit?
Thomas   Oh, certainly I hoped that it would be more of a religious experience than a holiday. I suppose I hoped that by following in Jesus' footsteps I could in some way get closer to him. Also I think I hoped that it would make the events of the Gospel story more real somehow.

And did the visit live up to expectations?
Thomas   Does anything?! It wasn't quite what I expected – at least not at first. For one thing – and this was really stupid of me – I hadn't realised how very *eastern* the country was. We see all these pictures of Jesus looking like a typical English gent. But one of the first things which impressed me was the fact that he must have looked much like the Arab and native Israeli population there now. We're so used to seeing Jesus and the Gospel characters played by Robert Powell, John Gielgud, Lawrence Olivier and so on – it's terribly deceptive! So I learnt that the image of Jesus which I carry in my mind's eye is just his image as I want to see him. One interesting thing I saw was at the Church in Nazareth. All around the courtyard are mosaics donated by countries from all over the world. The theme of each picture is the Virgin and child. Yet each mosaic portrays them with the characteristics of the nation involved. So the Chinese Virgin and child look Chinese; the Russians are in Russian traditional costume, and so on. I thought Bethlehem was a bit disappointing – it's quite a tourist trap, and I didn't think there was much of an atmosphere there. But people I spoke to say it's quite different at Christmas. Then Manger Square is crowded with pilgrims, and they say there is a wonderful feeling about the place, as though something important

really happened there. I loved Galilee. You can sit on the hills overlooking the sea of Galilee and just imagine what it was like in the time of Jesus. If you squint a bit, you can forget that the boats on the sea are modern motor boats, and can picture Peter and Andrew, James and John, in their fishing boats. There are modern towns around the seashore, but for the most part I should think that if Jesus came back tomorrow, he'd recognise where he was at once.

Did you feel the same way about Jerusalem?
Thomas   Jerusalem! Oh no! It's a magnetic place. When you're there, you know that you are somewhere special. The whole city shouts 'religion' at you from every corner. It is of course a holy city for Christians, Jews and Muslims, and you experience it all – the muezzin calling the Muslims to prayer in the morning; the Jews praying at the Western Wall. What made it very special for me was that we went at Easter. We arrived in Jerusalem on Maundy Thursday, and immediately visited the site of the Upper Room where Jesus held the Last Supper the night before he was killed. Then we went to Mass. The next day, Good Friday, we got up early and went to the beginning of the Via Dolorosa. This is the route which covers a number of roads, which Jesus followed from Pilate's judgement hall to the place of crucifixion, now in the Church of the Holy Sepulchre. We had arranged to collect a large wooden cross, and we walked along the route taking it in turns to carry it. All along the route were marked the stations of the cross. We stopped at each one and said prayers. This was really special to me, because in our Church we have the stations of the cross all round the walls, and on Good Friday at home we process around the Church stopping at each of the stations. We have one, for example, which recalls the place where Simon of Cyrene carried the cross, and here I was at the actual spot where it happened.

But Jerusalem has changed so much since the time of Jesus. No one really knows where he was crucified. Does it matter to you that many of the sites are 'traditional' rather than 'historical'?
Thomas   No, not really. After all, they've certainly got the starting point right because archaeologists have dug up The Antonia Fortress where Jesus was tried before Pilate. One of the most beautiful spots for me was underground. Beneath a convent they have found part of the original pavement of Pilate's palace, and you can be pretty sure that Jesus was very near to that spot. We know where the walls of the city were at the time, so nowhere on the route can be far out! Besides, how can I explain it; it doesn't matter whether this is the *exact* spot where Jesus fell. What is important is that by tracing his steps on that last terrible walk, we are remembering his sufferings for us, and I suppose in a way, sharing in them.

What was Easter Day like?

Thomas   Again, it didn't match up to my preconceptions. Of course most of the old city of Jerusalem is Arab, and any Sunday is much the same as any other day of the week. We are so used to Easter Day being a quiet English Spring day. This was an ordinary noisy, hot, bustling day in Jerusalem and, I dare say, much as it was on the day of the Resurrection. Of course there were crowds of pilgrims everywhere. One thing I did which was very special – I walked to the garden tomb very early – just as Mary Magdalene had done. I don't think anyone believes that it is the tomb of Jesus, but it dates from the same period and would be of the same type as the one he was buried in. All my illusions of having a quiet private moment were of course shattered! Half the city seemed to be there! But it didn't matter. It is a peaceful spot, and everyone there was quietly experiencing the moment for him or herself. That was actually rather important; knowing that my private thoughts were being shared by all those other people, in different languages and from all over the world. I am sure that like me, most of them were picturing Mary ariving at the tomb and finding the stone rolled away – then running to find the disciples with the wonderful news, 'He is risen!'

He has travelled halfway across the world to be here. Now he stands on the spot where Jesus is said to have spoken the Sermon on the Mount (see Matthew 5–7).
  What is going through his mind?

The Archbishop of Canterbury and other bishops have gone on pilgrimages to
Walsingham in Norfolk. In 1061 a woman in the village had a vision of the Virgin
Mary. Walsingham then became one of the most important pilgrimage centres in
Europe. Today it is a place of pilgrimage for Roman Catholics, Orthodox and
Anglicans. Many Protestants (including a number of Anglicans) do not approve of
these pilgrimages, especially since people who go on them usually offer prayers to
the Virgin. They also disapprove of shops which make money out of selling souvenirs,
such as statues of Mary.

Activity – discussion and writing

1   Write down the names of any special pilgrimage places in Israel
mentioned by Thomas. What events in the past made those places
famous?
2   What things surprised Thomas during his visit?
3   What reasons does Thomas give throughout his story for wanting to
go to Israel?
4   For what religions is Jerusalem a Holy City?
5   Why was it so special for Thomas to be in Jerusalem over the Easter
period?
6   Why do you think Thomas and the other pilgrims carried crosses
along the Via Dolorosa?
7   In what ways did the Via Dolorosa remind Thomas of his Church
back home?
8   Why was the visit to the Garden Tomb so special for Thomas?
9   Why do you think that artists so often portray Jesus with the features
of their own people?
10   What do you think Thomas learnt from his pilgrimage? Do you
think it was worthwhile from his point of view?
11   Write down a list of the differences between a pilgrimage and a
holiday.
12   Having read Thomas' story, would you be interested in going to
Israel? If so, what would you like to see there? Would you be going on
a pilgrimage or on a holiday?

Another famous pilgrimage centre is Lourdes *in France. This is another place where a girl had a vision of the Virgin. Lourdes is now particularly famous as a place of healing. (See Chapter 6.)*

One of the most ancient places of pilgrimage is Rome. Rome owes its importance to the tradition that the apostles Peter and Paul both preached and were put to death in the city. Roman Catholics especially believe that Peter was the first bishop of Rome, and that all bishops of Rome (popes) are his successors and have inherited his authority as leader of the Church. On Easter Day the Pope appears on the balcony of St Peter's and gives his blessing to the world. This event is always televised these days.

Prayer

What the New Testament says about prayer
The teaching of Jesus which is to be found in the Gospels, and the teaching of these and the other New Testament books are the foundation of the Christian faith.

Coursework (Knowledge)
Find out what the New Testament says about prayer. Read the following passages carefully and make notes under the following headings:
Are any special garments to be worn?
Where to pray.
Who/what to pray for.
How to/not to pray.
Who to pray to.
What happens during prayer?
What to say.
How many people need to pray together?
Reasons for prayer.
Actions accompanying prayer.

Passages for study
Matthew 5:44; 6:5–6, 7–9; 18:20; 19:13; 21:22; 26:39.
Mark 11:25; 14:22–25.
Luke 18:1–8, 9–14.
Acts 2:42; 6:4; 16:12–13; 21:5–6; 28:8.
Romans 8:26–27.
I Corinthians 11:4–11; 14:13–19.
Ephesians 5:18–20; 6:18–19.
Colossians 1:3.
If you find one of these passages too difficult for you, go on to the next one.
For your coursework, write up your notes under the above headings. Wherever possible, use your own words rather than copying from the text, except where you are quoting the words of an actual prayer.

We have seen that the word 'pilgrimage' is normally used to describe a physical journey. But many Christians see the whole of life as a pilgrimage – the pilgrimage of the soul. One of the most famous books in English is *The Pilgrim's Progress* by John Bunyan. The book tells of the journey of the pilgrims Christian and Hopeful on their way to the 'Eternal City'. On their way they meet many who try to prevent their progress, such as Obstinante, Worldly Wiseman, and Hypocrisy and others like Piety and Charity who help them on their way. Although written in the seventeenth century, this book is still published and read by many Christians who find in it guidance as to how to follow the Christian path in a world full of distractions and doubt.

Another book on a similar theme is *The Way of a Pilgrim*. This was written by an unknown nineteenth-century Russian peasant who, having lost everything, dedicates his life to finding the answer to the question 'how can a person pray unceasingly?'. The book is a guide to prayer, and is especially popular among Orthodox Christians.

Formal prayer

Daily prayer is an important activity for most Christians. Some like to use prayers which have been composed by other people and which they have learnt, or have in private prayer books. The most commonly-used prayer which every Christian knows is 'Our Father . . .' which Jesus himself taught his followers.

Most formal Christian prayers end with words such as 'In the name of Jesus Christ our Lord'. The word 'Amen' at the end of prayers simply means 'So let it be.'

Orthodox

Most Orthodox homes have at least one place of prayer where the family, or individuals gather each day. The central point of this place will be an icon. There will often be readings from the Bible, and sometimes rosaries will be used, and candles.

Roman Catholic

The Roman Catholic Church also teaches its children to use set prayers. The most popular of these is the Rosary. Each part of the Rosary reminds the bearer of an incident, or 'mystery' in the life of Jesus or Mary. While meditating on these incidents, the Our Father is said once and the 'Hail Mary' ten times.

Hail Mary, full of grace, the Lord is with thee
Blessed art thou among women, and blessed is the fruit of thy womb, Jesus
*   Christ.*
Holy Mary, Mother of God, pray for us sinners now and in the hour of our
*   death.*

Other famous prayers include:

(a) The Lord's Prayer

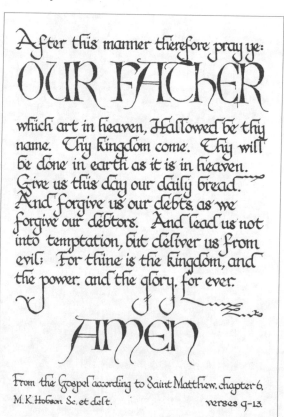

After this manner therefore pray ye:
OUR FATHER
which art in heaven, Hallowed be thy name. Thy kingdom come. Thy will be done in earth as it is in heaven. Give us this day our daily bread. And forgive us our debts, as we forgive our debtors. And lead us not into temptation, but deliver us from evil; For thine is the kingdom, and the power, and the glory, for ever.
AMEN

From the Gospel according to Saint Matthew. Chapter 6,
M. K. Hobson Sc. et delt.   verses 9–13.

(b) Francis of Assisi

Lord, make me an instrument of your
   peace:
where there is hatred, let me sow love:
where there is injury, pardon:
where there is doubt, faith:
where there is darkness, light:
where there is despair, hope,
and where there is sadness, joy.

Divine Master, grant that I may not so
   much seek
to be consoled as to console,
to be understood as to understand,
to be loved as to love.
For it is in giving that we receive,
it is in pardoning that we are pardoned,
and in dying that we are born to eternal
   life.

Prayer of Francis of Assisi

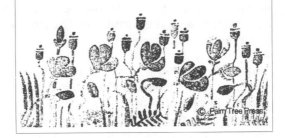

(c) The Evening Collect

Lighten our darkness we beseech thee O Lord;
And by thy great mercy, defend us from all the perils and dangers of this
   night,
For the Love of thy only Son, our Saviour, Jesus Christ.
Amen.

(d) The Jesus Prayer

Lord Jesus Christ, Son of God, have mercy on me a sinner.

Display work
Ask any Christians you know to write out for you their favourite prayer.
Make a collage of all the prayers your class collects, and also pictures
of books or objects which people might use to help them pray.

Spontaneous prayer
It would be quite wrong to think that Christians (or indeed people of
other faiths) always pray 'formally', at set times and using set prayers.

Here are some of the comments about prayer made by teenagers taking part in a weekly discussion group.

I usually pray as I go to school in the morning.

I don't 'say my prayers' as such, either in the morning or in the evening. But I certainly do pray every day. I might be standing at the bus stop when something important comes into my mind; so I talk to God about it. Or I might see someone who looks sad or ill, so I pray about them. You never know what you're going to pray about until it crops up!

I get really irritated by people who say that there's no point in praying, or that they've never heard God talking to them. They say that If God knows everything and can do anything, there's no point in praying because he knows what you're going to say anyway and can do it without you asking. That's missing the point as I see it. Praying — talking to God – is like communicating with another person. You can't know someone or have a relationship with them unless you talk to them and take the trouble to get to know them. As for not hearing God talk to you – I could name quite a lot of people in my class who sit through a whole lesson not hearing anything the teacher has said. It doesn't mean the teacher hasn't said anything! I don't mean that when you hear God 'speaking' to you, you actually hear a voice. That's what people who have no experience of prayer find difficult. You have to become sensitive to a different sort of communication which does not use human speech.

I've thought really hard about this question, 'why bother to pray since God knows and can do everything anyway?' I've worked out an answer that makes sense to me – whether it will to anyone else I don't know. I think it's all to do with the fact that God put our destiny in our own hands by giving us free will. I believe that God has an intention for the universe — a purpose if you like. One of the most exciting mysteries of life for me is what the human race is supposed to be like. If God intended us to be in his own image, we obviously haven't got there yet! Not by a long way! God has, and is, tremendous power. I think that he means us to be able to use that power. It is a power to be used only for good. I think that by praying we are sort of tapping that power, rather like when a house is connected to the mains for electricity. So some people have developed the gift of healing through prayer. I don't believe that God could not cure those people anyway. But if he did, all the time, the next step would be to miraculously stop a lorry that was about to run over a child – or he could have stopped that man who shot all those people; you could go on and on. But if God stopped all the bad things before they happened, think what our lives would be like. We wouldn't have any decisions to make, nothing to learn. We'd be like robots. I think that God expects us to solve the problems in the world, and learn from the things that go wrong. I think that he has given us the power of prayer to help 'tap' this massive force which most people are hardly aware of. I also think that the human race has only just begun to learn how to use this force.

The power of prayer
The following extracts from books are all about prayer.

What is the essence of prayer? . . . From general reading one gets the ideas about the external acts of piety and concludes that to pray it is necessary to go to Church, to make the sign of the cross, make prostrations, kneel, read the psalter. . . . I choose to think about every word of a prayer before I vocalise it. Prayer without interior feeling is not very effective either for the one who recites it or for the one who listens to it; everything depends on interior life and on attentive prayer. Of course God does not need prayer from us sinners, but in his love for us, he likes to see us pray. . . . God in his love, rewards man a thousand times more than his actions deserve. If you will give God a mite, then he will give you a gold piece. If you will only decide to say go to your Father, He will come to meet you.

from *The Way of the Pilgrim*

I knew God would provide for me, but as the family in Lung Kong Road grew I was amazed to see our income grow too. Ever since I had stopped teaching full-time I found that I received all that I needed. I was able to pay for the rent, the Youth Club room and my language lessons. Sometimes a cheque would arrive in the post. Sometimes a friend would give exactly the same amount as I had been praying for. When I wanted to buy a rubber boat for a swimming expedition with the boys, a friend sent the right sum from England without knowing the need. Now while we never had enough money to pay for the next week's food or rent, we always had enough for each day. This was exhilarating for the boys who felt they had a real part in God's work when they prayed each morning for their daily bread. Sometimes an anonymous sack of rice would appear on the doorstep; on one occasion it was a coffee table.

Every Sunday after the morning meeting we invited many people to lunch with us all at Lung Kong Road. A number of guests needed the good meal so it was sad when one Sunday I had to tell the boys that we had no money for food.

'Boil the rice anyway and we'll pray for something to put on top,' I said. Ten minutes before lunch a panting and sweating visitor arrived carrying tins of food and fresh bean sprouts. His Kowloon Bible class had made a collection for us on the spur of the moment and sent him with their gifts. The young man, William, enjoyed being an answer to prayer just as much as thirty of us enjoyed the huge meal only ten minutes later. It was an exciting way of life.

A delightful American sailor once took me to task about my praying in tongues. He thought I went on about it far too much. He had this gift himself, but he felt it should only be used sparingly for spiritual highs and for special occasions. I explained to him that one reason why God was able to use me was because I kept in touch through using this gift all the time. I prayed in the Spirit as I went around the Colony – in buses, on the boats, and walking along the streets, very quietly under my breath. That way it is possible to pray all the time. I offered, if he had time, to take him on a day-long tour of Hong Kong while we prayed continuously.

The next day we met up and walked down through Western District to the waterfront. The route reminded me of my first few days in Hong Kong when I began to see beneath the tourists' glamorous facade to the dirt, poverty and struggle, the ceaseless work and more work.

In one steep stepped ladder-street I passed an old man living in a cupboard five feet high, six feet long and three feet deep. He sold vegetables from his cupboard by day and climbed on top of them to sleep at night as there was nowhere else for him to live. With four and a half million people crammed into every available square foot, whole families in Hong Kong had to live in one room: this man had no family.

Further down the street I found an old lady holding out a plastic rice bowl. No one in Hong Kong had money or rooms to spare and there were no pensions either so she stayed alive by begging. There were so few old people's homes that she had not a hope of getting into one.

Walking on I saw a little girl of about five years old with a child strapped on her back, because both of her parents had to work long hours to support their children. Nobody looked after the dirty little five year old – she was looking after the baby.

Then I passed a teenage boy who paid rent for the privilege of sleeping on a four-foot shop counter. He had stopped school at the end of his primary years when he was about thirteen. He was bright and wanted to continue school but his parents took him away to work. When he got his job he gave all his money to them so that they could send all his younger brothers and sisters to school. Every time I walked past him he asked me to practise English with him to help him to get a better job.

I reached the end of the street feeling that if I spent my entire life down there I could just about get to love this street – I could just about get to love all the people and know them and their needs. But when we turned into the next street, it was a duplicate of the first and beyond that yet another. More people . . . I told the American sailor how I had prayed during the early days asking God to show me which bit of His work was mine; He had answered by sending me to the Walled City, and the miraculous events of the next dozen years. I could never have dreamed of anything so extraordinary and wonderful.

My sailor was as overwhelmed by this sight of Hong Kong as I had been. But the purpose of our day was to encourage him to walk in the Spirit so I began to pray as we went. We crossed the harbour and arrived at Jordan Road, an area I knew well as I had lived there for a while. I took him inside a building that boasted both brothels and ballrooms. It was a place where heroin addicts hung out, looking deathly sick and half-starved. We walked up the back staircase; there were various people sleeping on the stairs and we picked our way over the bodies, looking for a large tramp. I had come to find Mau Wong, the 'King of the Cats'; he was much fatter than the others there because he was a 'protector' for various prostitutes, and so earned quite a lot of money.

We found Mau Wong in an extremely unhappy state: he had a terrible stomach-ache and was sweating profusely and retching. He could not listen to me telling him about Jesus, so the young American and I laid hands upon him and prayed quietly in the Spirit for his healing. Very quickly his pain vanished, and a look of great surprise crossed his features. He could hardly believe what had happened to him, but he was now ready to sit down and listen. He accepted Jesus, and was baptized in the Spirit then and there. We had hardly finished praying when he got up, ran away and reappeared bringing with him a pathetic specimen of a man with sunken cheeks. Mau Wong explained that this friend had tooth-ache; would we pray for him too? So we took him up onto the roof of the building which was flat and empty and prayed with him also. He was healed at once, then we told him who Jesus was and what Jesus had done for him. He was ready to receive Christ and His Spirit and did so straight away. Then I had a message in tongues, and Mau Wong, the 'King of the Cats', was able to give the interpretation about repentance which thrilled him very much.

I was to visit Mau Wong on the back staircase several times to tell him more about Jesus; the second time I met him he gave me a knife and various equipment for smoking heroin, which he asked me to dispose of. He explained that now he was a Christian he had to earn his living in an honest way, so he had bought some shoe brushes, and was going to become a bootblack.

The young American and I left Mau Wong to continue our tour of Hong Kong; we crossed back over the harbour and took a minibus to Chaiwan. All the time I was praying aloud but quietly so that no one could hear. My sailor had thought that praying on buses was a bit much but after seeing what had happened at Jordan Road he began to join in too. The whole day we prayed without ceasing except to eat and to talk to those we met along the way.

from *Chasing the Dragon* by Jackie Pullinger

Professor B introduced me to his son, Janos. I instantly liked him. He had recently married and was doing well as a young attorney, and yet he too was willing to place his career on the line by taking part in these frowned-upon meetings of Christians. There were seven of us that night, seven Christians gathered in much the same way Christians had gathered since the Church began – in secret, in trouble – praying together that through the miraculous intervention of God Himself we be spared a confrontation with the authorities.

We prayed there in the living-room of Professor B, all kneeling around a low round coffee table in the centre of the room. For an hour we kept up an earnest intercession, begging God to help us in our time of need. And all at once, the praying stopped. To every one of us at the same instant came the inexplicable certainty that God had heard, that our prayer was answered.

We got up from our knees, blinking at each other in surprise. I looked at my watch. It was 11.35 in the evening. At that precise hour we *knew* that tomorrow everything was going to be all right.

from *God's Smuggler* by Brother Andrew

Talking about prayer

1   Find out if anyone you know can tell you more about 'praying in tongues'.
2   Jackie Pullinger and Brother Andrew both write about living a life of prayer – that is, putting themselves completely into God's hands and trusting that he will supply their needs. What is your reaction to what they say about this?
3   Try to get Christians you know to talk to you about their prayer lives (when they pray, what they pray for, why they pray, what good they think it does). Don't put pressure on people to talk about this. For some people it is a very personal matter and they may not feel at ease discussing it. If you do get any information, share it with others in your class.

Bible study

Many Christians read the Bible daily, and some use booklets which contain notes on the text for each day. Read Matthew 5:38–48 and the following notes.

SATURDAY JULY 25
MATTHEW 5:38–48
IN A CHRIST-REJECTING WORLD SOME HOSTILITY IS INEVITABLE.

Jesus knew his disciples would certainly meet 'evil persons' and suffer from physical abuse (39), emotional hurt ('slap you on the right cheek,' NEB), legal action, material deprivation (40), social pressure, and restricted freedom (41).

Exod 21:24

We must certainly not retaliate physically – remember that 'eye for an eye' was initially a limitation on revenge, not a licence to indulge in it. Neither can we be content simply with non-resistance, hard as that may be. Something more is demanded; in our dealings with others, cruel or kind, we need to be:

Generous. In their caring, believers must be as impartial as their heavenly Father (45). Set in this particular context it sounds as if the beggars and borrowers mentioned here (42) may be demanding what one is not really in a position to give or lend. This text must not be made into a new Christian law of utterly indiscriminate giving. We must be wise stewards as well as generous neighbours.

Compassionate. The 'hate your enemy' part of the quotation will not be found in Scripture. It may be an example of a scribal interpretation which rigidly limited Leviticus 19:18 to Israelites (thereby excluding Samaritans, Gentiles or enemies) and ignored other Old Testament injunctions about kindness to enemies.

Exod 23:4–5
Prov 25:21

Prayerful. True love cannot remain on the emotional level; it needs to do something. It can pray and it must. Dietrich Bonhoeffer (executed in a Nazi concentration camp) wrote: 'Through the medium of prayer we go to our enemy, stand by his side, and plead for him to God.'

Isa 51:6
1 Pet 2:23
Eph 5:18

If we are to outdo pagans in loving (46–47) and be worthy of our sonship (45), we must constantly recall the Father's generosity (45b) and nature (48), the Son's example, and the Spirit's power to make all this possible.

> ### Write your own
> Read Matthew 6:1–15 on prayer. Write your own study notes which you think might help other people to understand and think about what this passage means.

Resources

Books
J. R. Bailey, *Worship, Ceremonial and Rites of Passage* (Schofield & Sims)
H. Chicken, *Worship Among Us* (Longman)
Collinson & Miller, *Believers* (Arnold)
J. Rankin, *Looking at Worship* (Chichester Project) (Lutterworth)
D. Sullivan, *Visiting a Roman Catholic Church* (Lutterworth)
S. Tompkins, *Visiting an Anglican Church* (Lutterworth)
M. Ward, *Protestant Christian Churches* (Ward Lock)
K. Weitzman, *The Icon* (Chatto & Windus)
K. Weitzman, *Journeys into Religion* (Schools Council)
K. Weitzman, *Religion in Britain Today* (Schools Council)
R. St L. Broadberry, *Thinking about Christianity* (Lutterworth)
J. Rankin, *The Eucharist* (Chichester Project) (Lutterworth)
J. Rankin, *Christian Worship* (Chichester Project) (Lutterworth)
J. Bates, *Visiting a Methodist Church* (Lutterworth)

Texts
The Missal; The Alternative Service Book; Hymn Books; Prayer Books; *The Way of the Pilgrim*

Audio-visual aids
From the Slide Centre:
   S1411 *Christian Worship – Anglican*
   S1416 *Christian Worship – Baptist*
   S1464 *Christian Churches*
   S1465 *Christian Symbols*
Videotext, *Aspects of Christianity*

5 Living a Christian life

What I think is . . .

Activity 1

Tell a friend briefly your opinion on the following:

(a) the death penalty

(b) unemployment

(c) abortion.

Now make a note of what you both said.

Look carefully at what you have written, and think carefully about what your partner said. These three issues are very sensitive ones, and you may well have strong feelings and opinions on all of them. But where did those opinions come from? Thin air? Did you reason them through, weighing up the evidence? Did the answers seem in some way to be 'common sense'? Were you repeating opinions you had heard?

None of us work out our attitudes without reference to the beliefs and attitudes of others. But what are the influences around us which help to form our attitudes and opinions?

Activity 2

Here is a list of possible influences on our lives.

PARENTS   OTHER FAMILY MEMBERS   PRESS   TV

INSTINCT   FRIENDS   SCHOOL   REASON

STUDY AND KNOWLEDGE   RELIGION   EMOTION   RADIO

Indicate the effect that each of these factors has on your life on a scale of 1 to 5. So, if you think that the views of your parents influence you very much indeed, put 5 against parents. You might want to list other things which you or someone in your group thinks influences our decision-making.

Sticking to the rules

In 1924 the Olympic Games were held in Paris. The British team went to the games with high hopes of a gold medal in the 100 metres sprint – their hopes were centred on a Scottish runner and rugby player called Eric Liddel.

Liddel seemed unbeatable, but then something quite unforeseen happened. It was announced that the heats for both the 100 metres *and* the 4 × 100 metres relay were to be run on a Sunday. Like many other Scottish families, the Liddels believed firmly that the Sabbath was God's day. Playing rugby and running were not the sort of things that a Christian should be doing on the Sabbath. Liddel refused.

Very few people could understand it. Some called him a traitor, and there were letters and articles in the newspapers suggesting that he should change his mind. But he still would not run.

However, Liddel did run in the 400 metres, a race for which he had not trained and with which he was not familiar. When he reached the track, Liddel read a note that had been handed him by the masseur. It said, 'It says in the good book, "He who honours me, I will honour." Good Luck'. Liddel won the gold medal.

'God made me fast; and when I run, I feel his pleasure.'

Top: Eric Liddel

Below: a scene from the film Chariots of Fire, *which was based on Liddel's life.*

> **Something to discuss and write about**
>
> Discuss the following questions, giving clear reasons for your point of view.
>
> 1   Where in the Bible would Liddel have found the teaching about the Sabbath which he kept so strictly?
>
> 2   What does Liddel's decision tell us about his attitude towards the Bible and the teaching of his Church?
>
> 3   Was Liddel's attitude selfish – putting his personal principles before the common cause?
>
> 4   Were the press justified in putting so much pressure on him?
>
> 5   If Liddel *had* run, what do you think
>   (a) other people would have said about him
>   (b) he would have thought about himself?
>
> 6   Can you find any stories from recent times about people who have refused to take part in something on their holy day?
>
> 7   Do you think that most Christians today have the same attitude towards the Bible and its teaching as Liddel did? How might you find out?

Read this passage from *The Hiding Place* by Corrie ten Boom. Corrie lived in Haarlem in Holland at the time of the German invasion in the Second World War. Her family was one of many which risked their lives by hiding Jews in their house. One day, Corrie was summoned to the police station. She packed her 'prison bag' expecting to be arrested. . . .

A matter of conscience

The policeman on duty was an old acquaintance. He looked at the letter, then at me with curious expression. 'This way,' he said.

He knocked at a door marked 'Chief.' The man who sat behind the desk had red-grey hair combed forward over a bald spot. A radio was playing. The chief reached over and twisted the volume knob not down but up.

'Miss ten Boom,' he said. 'Welcome.'

'How do you do, Sir.'

The chief had left his desk to shut the door behind me. 'Do sit down,' he said. 'I know all about you, you know. About your work.'

'The watchmaking you mean. You're probably thinking more about my father's work than my own.'

The chief smiled. 'No, I mean your "other" work.'

'Ah, then you're referring to my work with retarded children? Yes. Let me tell you about that—'

'No, Miss ten Boom,' the chief lowered his voice. 'I am not talking about your work with retarded children. I'm talking about still another work, and I want you to know that some of us here are in sympathy.'

The chief was smiling broadly now. Tentatively I smiled back. 'Now, Miss ten Boom,' he went on, 'I have a request.'

The chief sat down on the edge of his desk and looked at me steadily. He dropped his voice until it was just audible. He was, he said, working with the underground himself. But an informer in the police department was leaking information to the Gestapo. 'There's no way for us to deal with this man but to kill him.'

A shudder went down my spine.

'What alternative have we?' the chief went on in a whisper. 'We can't arrest him – there are no prisons except those controlled by the Germans. But if he remains at large many others will die. That is why I wondered, Miss ten Boom, if in your work *you* might know of someone who could—'

'Kill him?'

'Yes.'

I leaned back. Was this all a trap to trick me into admitting the existence of a group, into naming names?

'Sir,' I said at last, seeing the chief's eyes flicker impatiently, 'I have always believed that it was my role to save life, not destroy it. I understand your dilemma, however, and I have a suggestion. Are you a praying man?'

'Aren't we all, these days?'

'Then let us pray together now that God will reach the heart of this man so that he does not continue to betray his countrymen.'

There was a long pause. Then the chief nodded. 'That I would very much like to do.'

And so there in the heart of the police station, with the radio blaring out the latest news of the German advance, we prayed. We prayed that this Dutchman would come to realise his worth in the sight of God and the worth of every other human being on earth.

Questions for discussion

1 Corrie was sticking to a principle which she had been taught from the Bible. Where in the Bible would she have read this principle?
2 Imagine that you were Corrie. Write down the arguments (from her point of view) for and against arranging the man's death.
3 What does her decision tell you about Corrie?
4 'There are times when a conscience is an extravagant luxury which you just can't afford'. Do you think that this is true? Was this one of those occasions?

The lie

We were chatting in the kitchen with Cocky and Katrien when all at once Peter and his older brother, Bob, raced into the room, their faces white. 'Soldiers! Quick! They're two doors down and coming this way!'

They jerked the table back, snatched away the rug and tugged open the trapdoor. Bob lowered himself first, lying down flat, and Peter tumbled in on top of him. We dropped the door shut, yanked the rug over it and pulled the table back in place. With trembling hands Betsie, Cocky, and I threw a long tablecloth over it and started laying five places for tea.

There was a crash in the hall as the front door burst open and a smaller crash close by as Cocky dropped a teacup. Two uniformed Germans ran into the kitchen, rifles levelled.

'Stay where you are. Do not move.'

We heard boots storming up the stairs. The soldiers glanced around disgustedly at this room filled with women and one old man. If they had looked closer at Katrien she would surely have given herself away: her face was a mask of terror. But they had other things on their minds.

'Where are your men?' the shorter soldier asked Cocky in clumsy, thick-accented Dutch.

'These are my aunts,' she said, 'and this is my grandfather. My father is at his school, and my mother is shopping, and—'

'I didn't ask about the whole tribe!' the man exploded in German. Then in Dutch: 'Where are your brothers?'

Cocky stared at him a second, then dropped her eyes. My heart stood still. I knew how Nollie had trained her children – but surely, surely now of all times a lie was permissible!

'Do you have brothers?' the officer asked again.

'Yes,' Cocky said softly. 'We have three.'

'How old are they?'

'Twenty-one, nineteen, and eighteen.'

Upstairs we heard the sounds of doors opening and shutting, the scrape of furniture dragged from walls.

'Where are they now?' the soldier persisted.

Cocky leaned down and began gathering up the broken bits of cup. The man jerked her upright. 'Where are your brothers?'

'The oldest one is at the Theological College. He doesn't get home most nights because – '

'What about the other two?'

Cocky did not miss a breath.

'Why, they're under the table.'

Motioning us all away from it with his gun, the soldier seized a corner of the cloth. At a nod from him the taller man crouched with his rifle cocked. Then he flung back the cloth.

At last the pent-up tension exploded: Cocky burst into spasms of high hysterical laughter. The soldiers whirled around. Was this girl laughing at them?

'Don't take us for fools!' the short one snarled. Furiously he strode from the room and minutes later the entire squad trooped out – not, unfortunately, before the silent soldiers had spied and pocketed our precious packet of tea.

Something to discuss and write about

1 Would you bring your children up to tell the truth at all times?
2 Are there any times when it is justifiable to tell a lie? Do you think that the occasion you have just read about was one of them?
3 Which of the following words do you think describe Cocky's reply to the soldier: foolish / clever / irresponsible / disloyal / honest?
4 Nollie taught her children to tell the truth always. Where did she find this rule in the Bible?
5 What would you say the central characters in these three stories had in common?

As you probably realised, they all regarded the Bible teaching as absolutely binding on their lives. They looked to the Bible for instructions as to how to live their lives, and did not break the laws in the Bible under any circumstances. However, not all Christians look to the Bible to give them an answer to every problem in life.

This is what one famous Christian writer has to say.

A law provides security, because we know exactly what we have to keep to: just this, no less but no more. . . . But no law can envisage all possibilities, take into account all cases, fill all gaps. . . . The law does at least lay down clear limits. In particular cases there is still always room for discussion: Was it really adultery? . . . If perjury is against the law, does this not include all the more harmless forms of untruthfulness?

It is also easy to see why so many people prefer to keep the law with reference to God himself. For in this way I know exactly when I have done my duty. . . .

It is precisely this legalistic attitude, however, to which Jesus gives the *deathblow*. Man's relationship to God is not established by a code of law, without his being personally involved. He must submit himself, not simply to the law, but to God; to accept, that is, what God demands of him in a wholly personal way. . . . Each one must find for himself the application in his own life (of the law of love).

Hans Küng, *On Being a Christian*

The distinctive Christian feature . . . is not an abstract something . . . it is this concrete Jesus as the Christ, as the standard.

Something to discuss and write about

1 Try to explain in your own words what Hans Küng is saying are the *advantages* of living according to the letter of the law.
2 Try to explain in your own words what Hans Küng sees as the *disadvantages* of trying to live by the letter of the law.
3 What do you think Küng means when he says that Jesus Christ is the 'standard' for a Christian?

What the Bible says

The Ten Commandments
You probably realised that Liddel, Corrie and Cocky were all keeping very strictly one of the *Ten Commandments*. These ten laws form the basis of the law in the Old Testament.

Activity 3
You have already discovered three of the Ten Commandments. Can you, working in pairs, remember the other seven? Once you have reconstructed the list, put the Ten Commandments in order of importance as *you* see them. Check your list with the actual list in the Bible. Did you remember them correctly? How does the original order compare with yours?

> **Activity 4**
> Look up Mark 12:28–29 and/or Luke 10:25–28.
> What did Jesus say were the two greatest commandments?
> What would you say was the most important word which Jesus used to describe the two commandments?
> Now divide your book or filo paper into two vertical columns. Write out one of the two 'greatest commandments' at the top of each column. Now look again at the original Ten Commandments. Write each one down in one of your two columns.
> (You will have to decide which column each one should go in.)
> Now write a brief explanation of why Jesus said that these two commandments were the summary of all the commandments.

Love is . . . according to St Paul

Jesus said that *love* was the most important thing, and that to live one's life with a *loving* attitude towards God and towards other people was to live according to the will of God. He did not lay down any complicated rules like those in the Old Testament, but he did tell a number of stories which illustrated what he meant by 'Love' and also, by his own example, showed what he meant.

A man who became a Christian not long after the death of Jesus was St Paul. He travelled through many countries spreading the Christian message, and wrote many letters to the Churches he visited. In one of these letters – to the Church at Corinth – he wrote what was to become a very famous passage all about love. Here is the passage. Some of you may have heard it before. Some of the words are missing.

> **Activity 5**
> In groups of three or four, discuss which words you would put in the gaps. There are a number of possibilities for each, so don't be afraid of putting the wrong answer. Discuss your choice of words with the rest of the class.
>
> I may be able to speak the languages of men and even of angels, but if I have no love, my speech is no more than a noisy gong or a clanging bell. I may have the gift of inspired preaching; I may have all ——— and understand all ——— : I may have all the ——— needed to move mountains – but if I have no love, I am ——— . I may give away everything I have, and even give my body to be burnt – but if I have no love, this does me ——— good.
>
>   Love is ——— and ——— ; it is not ——— or ——— or ——— ; love is not ——— or ——— or ——— ; love does not keep a record of ——— ; love is not ——— with evil, but is happy with the ——— . Love never ——— ; and its faith, hope and patience never fail.
>
>   Love is ——— . There are inspired messages, but they are temporary; there are gifts of speaking in strange tongues, but they will cease; there is knowledge, but it will ——— . For our gifts of

knowledge and of inspired messages are only partial, but when it
is ——— comes, then what is partial will disappear.

When you have completed the activity, read the whole passage. (Use a
Concordance to find it.)
1   Draw three columns in your book. In the **first** column make a list of
the words which the class chose to describe what love is and is not.
Start each word with '*is*' or '*is not*'. In the **second** column write the words
which St Paul used to describe what love is and is not, and in the **third**
column write a word or phrase which means the same as Paul's word.
2   Paul said that certain things were no use without love. Make a list
of these things. What do you think he meant?
3   What do you think would be a good title for the passage?

The New Law

Activity 6
A   Read Matthew 5:1–12.
1   What does the word 'blessed' mean?
2   What qualities does the passage suggest are possessed by those
who are 'blessed'? Are these qualities which you admire?
3   What does Jesus say about his followers being persecuted for what
they believe? What does persecution mean?
B   Read Matthew 5:13–14.
Jesus compared his followers to *salt* and *light*. Explain in your own words
what he meant.
C   Read the following passage *without looking in your Bible*. You should
work with a partner.

You have heard that people were told in the past, 'Do not commit
murder; anyone who does will be brought to trial.' But now I tell you;
whoever is angry with his brother will be brought to trial, whoever calls
his brother 'You good-for-nothing!' will be brought before the Council,
and whoever calls his brother a worthless fool will be in danger of
going to the fire of hell. So if you are about to offer your gift to God
at the altar and there remember that your brother has something
against you, leave your gift there in front of the altar, go at once and
make peace with your brother, and then come back and offer your
gift to God. If someone brings a lawsuit against you and takes you
to court, settle the dispute with him while there is time, before you go
to court. Once you are there, he will hand you over to the judge, who
will hand you to the police, and you will be put in jail. There you will
stay, I tell you, until you pay the last penny of your fine. You have
heard that it was said, 'Do not commit adultery.' But now I tell you;
anyone who looks at a woman and wants to possess her is guilty of
committing adultery with her in his heart. So if your right eye causes
you to sin, take it out and throw it away. It is much better for you to
lose a part of your body than to have your whole body thrown into
hell. If your right hand causes you to sin, cut if off and throw it away!
It is much better for you to lose one of your limbs than to have your

whole body thrown into hell. It was also said, 'Anyone who divorces his wife must give her a written notice of divorce.' But now I tell you: If a man divorces his wife, for any cause other than unfaithfulness, then he is guilty of making her commit adultery if she marries again; and the man who marries her commits adultery also. You have also heard that people were told in the past, 'Do not break your promise, but do what you have vowed to the Lord to do.' But now I tell you: do not use any vow when you make a promise. Do not swear by heaven because it is God's throne; nor by earth, for it is the resting place for his feet; nor by Jerusalem for it is the city of the great King. Do not even swear by your head because you cannot make a single hair white or black. Just say 'Yes' or 'No' – anything else you say comes from the evil one. You have heard that it was said, 'An eye for an eye and a tooth for a tooth.' But now I tell you; do not take revenge on someone who wrongs you. If anyone slaps you on the right cheek, let him slap your left cheek too. And if anyone takes you to court to sue you for your shirt, let him have your coat as well. And if one of the occupation troops forces you to carry his pack for one kilometre, carry it two kilometres. When someone asks you for something, give it to him; when someone wants to borrow something, lend it to him. You have heard that it was said, 'Love your friends, hate your enemies.' But now I tell you: love your enemies and pray for those who persecute you, so that you may become the sons of your Father in heaven. For he makes his sun to shine on good and bad people alike, and gives rain to those who do good and those who do evil. Why should God reward you if you love only the people who love you? Even the tax collectors do that! And if you speak only to your friends, have you done anything out of the ordinary? Even the pagans do that! You must be perfect – just as your Father in heaven is perfect.

1   The passage falls into a number of sections. Make a note of where you think each section ends and another begins.
2   Now decide on a suitable title for each section. The titles should reflect the content of the sections.
3   Now, using a *Concordance*, find the passage in the Bible. See if your sections are the same as those in the original text. If there are any differences, see if you can work out how you reached your decision. Do you want to change that decision now?
4   Draw a table, as below.

Heading	Old law	New law	Example

In the left-hand column write down the headings you chose for the six sections. Now fill in *briefly* the details in the other columns, i.e. in the second column you note down what *was* said in the law, and in the third column, make notes about what *Jesus* said on each subject. In the

fourth column note any example given by Jesus to illustrate what he
meant. If there is no example, make up one of your own, but write it in
a different colour and make a note to show that it is your example.
D Read Matthew 6:24–34.
Make notes on this passage in the form of a diagram. You might choose
to complete this one.
E Read Matthew 7:24–29.
Present this parable in the form of cartoon pictures. Then briefly explain
what you think the parable means.
F Summary
You will by now have spent some time studying passages in the New
Testament which suggest certain standards of behaviour from followers
of Jesus. In the next chapter we will see how some Christians today try
to apply this teaching to modern issues.

1   Draw a summary diagram to illustrate those qualities which *should*
be characteristic of a Christian, and those qualities which should *not*
be characteristic of a Christian.

Characteristic of a Christian	Not characteristic of a Christian

2   Look at your diagram carefully. Which of the qualities suggested as
being those of a Christian do you think are still those of most Christians
today? Do you think any of these qualities are now 'out of date'? If so,
explain why you think so. Look at the qualities which, according to the
New Testament, Christians should not possess. Do you think that all
Christians today take these suggestions seriously? What sort of survey
might you conduct to find out if your conclusions are correct?
   Do you think that any of them are not strictly relevant to living a
Christian life?

Coursework (Understanding)

People studying music are often set an exercise in which they have
to compose a piece of music in the style of a certain composer. You
may have been asked by an English teacher also to compose a poem
in the style of a certain famous poet.

Your task now is to write a parable for today *in the style of Jesus*.
Take any of the themes which have appeared in this chapter so far,
and write a parable on that theme. Remember that Jesus used people
and objects in his parables which were commonplace in his time. In
your parable, tell the story as though it were being told by Jesus

today, not 2000 years ago. Some of the characters may be the same –
we still have kings, soldiers, and shepherds. But tax-collectors,
beggars and Samaritans are not commonplace. You will need to ask
yourself what sort of people and what sort of situations Jesus would
have used in his parables were he telling them today.

Coursework (K, U and E)

Snakes and Ladders
Your RE teacher might have a game of snakes and ladders produced
by a Muslim organisation to help Muslim children understand the
important moral teaching of their faith. (Ask for permission to copy
a small portion.)

Knowledge
Design a snakes-and-ladders board which could be used as the basis
of discussion about Christian values. Your board should have ten
snakes, all of different lengths, and ten ladders also of different
lengths. You have to make a list of *ten* positive Christian values for
today, i.e. think of ten ways in which Christians might put their
belief into practice in today's society. (You might say, for instance,
'Give all your pocket money to Crisis at Christmas'.) When you have
done this, try to put the ten actions into order of importance as you
see it. Then write each one at the foot of a ladder, the most important
at the foot of the longest ladder and the least important at the foot of
the shortest ladder. Then do the same with the snakes, only this time
choose ten actions which in your judgement would go against
Christian principles. Put the action which you consider to be furthest
from Christian principles at the top of the longest snake and so on
(e.g. stealing from a coat left in a classroom).

Understanding
Take five of your 'ladder' actions and five of your 'snake' actions.
Explain carefully why you chose them (you should refer to the
teaching of the New Testament) and why you put them in that order.

Evaluation
How useful do you think this game would be
(a) for teaching children about Christian principles?
(b) as a basis of discussion about Christian principles?

Resources

Books
B. Wintersgill, *Facing the Issues* (Macmillan)
C. Ericker, *Christian Ethics* (Chichester Project) (Lutterworth)
P. Mullen, *Ethics* (Arnold)
P. Mullen, *The Church and the Bomb* (Hodder)
Brother Andrew, *God's Smuggler* (Hodder)
J. Pullinger, *Chasing the Dragon* (Hodder)
C. ten Boom, *The Hiding Place* (Hodder)
D. Field, *Christianity in the Modern World* (Hulton)
H. Hay *The Quakers* (Ward Lock)
M. Chignell, *Framework* (Arnold)
R. Owen, *Christian Aid* (RMEP)
J. Mayled, *Let's Discuss Poverty* (Wayland)
M. Gibson, *Let's Discuss Unemployment* (Wayland)
May and Pead, *Let's Discuss Violence* (Wayland)
J. Stott, *Issues Facing Christians Today* (Marshall)

Audio-visual aids
Chariots of Fire
The Hiding Place
A Question of Faith CTVC
The Healing Ministry (Church's Council for Health and Healing)

6 Three issues for today

Objectives for Chapter 6

1   What you should KNOW.
Three particular issues which concern Christians today:
Work and leisure
War and peace
Health and wholeness.

2   What you should UNDERSTAND.
(a) *New words and technical terms*
Work; leisure; creation; fulfilment; creativity; self-esteem; equality; respect; rights; pacifism; just war; wholeness; healing.
(b) *People, writings and traditions*
(i) People. The importance of people in the Christian family who are concerned with these issues: e.g. industrial chaplains; hospital chaplains; people in the healing ministry; Quakers; Christian CND; HM Forces chaplains.
(ii) Writings: Biblical teaching on these issues.
(iii) Traditions. NB The 'ecumenical' nature of special ministries.
(c) *Belief*
e.g. the 'new life' ethic; the sanctity of life; the power of God.
(d) *Moral issues*
Attitudes to work and unemployment; pay; strikes; the use of violence; transplants; life-support machines.
(e) *Questions about the meaning of life*
e.g. Why do we work?
How do we gain self-esteem? Is killing people ever justified? Is there such a thing as spiritual healing? What do we mean by wholeness?

3   What you should be able to DO.
Evaluate on the basis of evidence and argument questions arising from the study of this chapter.

Talking pictures

On pages 154–56 are people engaged in activities. In each case say whether or not you would describe what they are doing as 'work'.

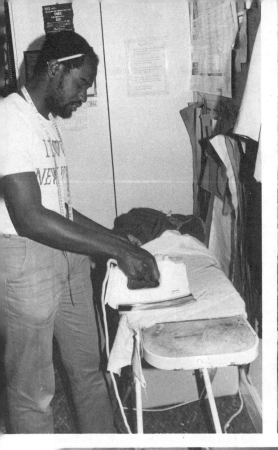

Now look at each picture again. Write down as many reasons as you can why the person/people in the pictures may be doing this task.

Discussion
The three quarrymen each have different attitudes to their work. Can you explain what 'work' means to each of them?

What are you doing?
I'm quarrying stone, what do you think I'm doing?

What are you doing?
I'm earning £100 p.w. mate. How about you?

What are you doing?
I'm building a cathedral.

Something to discuss and write about

A Here are some statements about work. In groups, discuss each statement. Make a note of the arguments for agreeing or disagreeing with the statement.

1 The job you do gives you your status in society.
2 People with better-paid jobs have more power in society than people with badly-paid jobs.
3 Some jobs are more important than others.
4 People who do important jobs are more important as people.
5 People who do not have a job do not contribute to society.
6 People who have jobs are entitled to a higher standard of living than people who do not.
7 To work is to pray. (St Benedict)
8 Working is not the same as having a job.
9 Everyone has the right to a job.
10 He who will not work, shall not eat.
11 Work is boring.
12 Work is to be avoided at all costs.
13 Women who stay at home, do housework and rear children, should be paid for doing so.

B Here are five more statements about work. Discuss them, and make sure that you understand what they mean. Do you agree with the attitudes expressed?

1 'I go on working for the same reason as a hen goes on laying eggs' (H. L. Mencken).
2 'Work is not primarily a thing one does to live, but the thing one lives to do' (Dorothy L. Sayers).
3 'Work is a good thing for a man . . . through it . . . he also achieves fulfilment as a human being, and indeed, in a sense, becomes more than a human being' (*Laborem Exercens*, John Paul).
4 'There is nothing better for a man than to enjoy his work' (Ecclesiastes 2:24).
5 'Work is the expenditure of energy (manual or mental or both) in the service of others, which brings fulfilment to the worker, benefit to the community, and glory to God' (John Stott, *Issues Facing Christians Today*).

Wall work

Let each group write a short definition of work. Display your definitions for the rest of the class to discuss.

A Christian view of work

The two Christian Creeds which you have been referring to while reading this book both describe God as 'maker of heaven and earth'. God is therefore seen as a *creative* being – a worker, you might say. Christian teaching also says that humanity was made 'in the image of God'. The Genesis story of the Creation says that Adam was given a job to do. He was to look after the Garden of Eden. This was a way of saying that human beings were given the Earth to tend and care for along with God. God did not create a world which looks after itself – a world where things 'just happen'.

Credo

I believe in God, the Father almighty, maker of heaven and Earth.

This child has been given materials – bricks, paints, etc. But the bricks will just be bricks until the child realises that something can be made from them.

Many Christians see the position of people on earth as being rather like the position of this child. We find ourselves in a massive 'playground' with a vast variety of materials to discover and use. The world which we and our ancestors have built is a result of our work with these materials. Like the children we have been given problems to solve, and intelligent minds to use in solving the problems.

This can be seen as a partnership between the human race and God. There are many wonders in the world for us to discover and · once we have discovered them, we have to decide how best to use them.

Gardener *Look 'ere, Vicar. See them delphiniums. I thought they was never goin'
to flower this year, considerin' the rain an' all. An' them dahlias too. Took months
for they to show their 'eads.*
Vicar *Indeed Harry, indeed. But doesn't that just show you what a wonderful world
the good Lord has given us? The flowers, the birds, the colours and textures. . . .*
Gardener *'Ere, steady on Vicar. I'm no denying the good Lord's presence an'all,
but he don't get all the credit. You should 'ave seen this 'ere garden when Gawd
had it all to 'isself.*

(Based on a story told by Basil Willey; from *Religion Today*, A. & C. Black,
1969)

What are you? Who are you?
Our society revolves around work. It is decided that certain jobs are
necessary in order for society to function. We all depend on each
other to work for each other. Many of us get a lot of satisfaction from
knowing that what we do benefits many other people. For many
people, having a job is important for their self-esteem.

Discussion
1   What do you understand by
    (a) job-satisfaction?
    (b) self-esteem?
2   What things have you done which have given you the greatest
satisfaction with yourself? (i.e. that made you feel good about yourself,
feel that you had achieved something). Perhaps the whole class could
make a display of things which have given individual members a sense
of achievement. Can you find any common points between these things?
(Were some of them difficult tasks which were carried out? or creative
tasks?)
3   In groups, make a list of the people who *work* for you during a year.
Select the ten which you feel to be making the most important
contribution to your lives (the ten whom you would miss the most if they
weren't there). Display your work for others to see.

Full marks!

Marcus Sieff, of Marks and Spencer fame, has published his autobiography. In it he gives an example of some enlightened personnel decisions. On one occasion a cleaner in a particular store who had twenty years' service was given a fortnight's leave to go to her son's wedding in South America – and the company paid her fare. In Sieff's own words:

I cited this as an example of 'good human relations at work' to the head of a major firm. He said, 'You must be mad to do it for a cleaner.' 'If', I asked, 'you had an executive in your organisation who, for some reason or other, was short of money and had a similar problem, would you not allow him the time off and give or loan him the money?' 'Ah,' he replied, 'an executive, that would be different. Yes, I would.' I said, 'Please tell me why such privileges should be given to an executive and not to a cleaner who has given many years of loyal and faithful service.' He did not give me a satisfactory answer.

(From *CURSOR Industrial Mission Newsletter* no. 16, Spring 1987, St Albans Diocese)

Work evaluation

This is an exercise where you think about what factors should influence the amount of money people are paid for doing a job.

1 Here is a table listing factors which apply to some jobs. Working with a partner, choose *five* of them which you consider should be taken into account when deciding how much a person should be paid.

	Shop assistant		Bank clerk		Nurse		Car mechanic		Teacher		Barrister	
A	x	y	x	y	x	y	x	y	x	y	x	y
length of service												
length of training												
skill												
concentration												
effort												
output / production												
responsibility for equipment												
responsibility for people												
bad conditions												
boredom												
antisocial hours												
contribution to national economy												
contribution to peoples' quality of life												
TOTAL SCORE												
ORDER												

2   Of the five factors you have chosen, decide which are the most important. Give each of the five a mark out of 5 and write the mark in column A.

3   Now look at each of the jobs in the top band. You must think about how important each of your five factors is in each job. So for each job, give each of your five factors a mark on the following basis.

5   absolutely essential
4   very important
3   important
2   useful
1   not important
0   unnecessary

Write the score for each job in column *x* for that job.

4   Taking each job in turn, for each factor, multiply the mark in column *A* by the score for that job in column *x* and write the result in column *y*.

5   Add up the scores for each job (i.e. the marks in column *y*) and enter the total.

6   Place the jobs in order according to their total scores.

7   Try to find out the actual wages for these jobs and compare with your decision. Discuss any differences between your order and the actual order. What could be the cause for any difference of opinion?

8   Some people suggest that there should be a national system, perhaps like the one you have been working out, for deciding on levels of pay on the basis of certain factors, so that everyone could understand why they were being paid a certain amount, and why someone else was being paid more or less. Do you think this is a good idea?

Industrial mission
Why is a Christian minister in the photo? What is he doing?

He is an *industrial chaplain*. Fifty years ago it was taken for granted that 'the people' would automatically come to 'the Church'. Today this is not the case, and fewer people have any direct contact with the Church. And yet the Church still feels that it has a lot to offer people, and also has to bear in mind the command of Jesus that his followers should 'go out into all the world' and preach the Gospel. Jesus also told his followers that their mission, like his own, was one of *service to others*.

It has been the custom for centuries for priests and ministers to visit people in their homes. But only in recent years has the Church begun to realise that the place where it can be of the most service to the most people is in their place of work, which is where so many people spend most of their time, and where many of their problems arise.

What does an industrial chaplain do?

Industrial chaplains are men and women from all denominations. Each area has a team. Some are priests and ministers; some are not. They are trained especially to visit workplaces and to get involved with activities centring on those places of work. Their aim is to make a contribution to the lives of people at work, be they 'workers' or 'management'.

An industrial chaplain *represents* the Church. He or she will visit a factory, an office, a power station, etc. and talk to the people there in an informal way, getting to know them and what they do. Most chaplains would say that they are especially concerned with relationships between people, and with people's dignity and self esteem. They might also think very carefully as someone 'coming in' from the outside, about how the institution they are visiting affects the lives of the people working in it. It would not be surprising therefore to find the chaplain being consulted by the company personnel manager, or by trade union leaders.

An industrial chaplain also has a *pastoral* role. He or she may be involved in training programmes for new members of a firm, and may be consulted by anyone working there about a personal problem. The chaplain is often seen as more approachable because he or she is not employed by the firm and can be guaranteed to keep a confidence.

Industrial chaplains also see their task as a *prophetic* one. By this they mean that they are sometimes able to see the implications of decisions and conflicts for the lives of individuals and for society as a whole. Sometimes the chaplain will be consulted over matters of firms' policy, about changes in structure and organisation. It is not unknown for a managing director who is a Christian to call in a team of industrial chaplains as consultants to suggest ways in which the firm can be run more on the lines of Christian principles.

Activities

1 Try to arrange for an industrial chaplain to talk to your class. You might also invite in someone from a local firm who allow the chaplain to come in and visit. Find out from both points of view what the chaplain contributes to the firm.

2 *Your* place of work is your school. You may have a school chaplain. If so, find out what his job involves. If not, discuss what contribution an industrial chaplain could make if he or she made regular visits to your school as a place of work. In what ways might this be of benefit to

(a) pupils,
(b) teachers,
(c) senior staff?

Coursework: a case study

Look at the 'Aims' of Industrial Mission in one area of the country.

The Aims

To understand industry and the way it affects people
To care for people working in industry
To help overcome barriers which prevent dialogue and mutual understanding
To help bring about the changes which may create a more humane and just society
To help the Church understand mission in urban industrial society

Bill is a chaplain with this team. He is very concerned about what he sees as a massive division in many places of work between the 'workers' and the 'bosses'. He is worried that a lot of people live their whole lives feeling insignificant and undervalued. Then, one day, an opportunity presents itself for him to do something about it. . . .

Tucked away in the back streets of the city is the firm of Smasher and Smasher, glassmakers. It is an old-established family firm (established 1856), currently doing very well financially. Theophilus Smasher, OBE, died last month, and has now been replaced as Managing Director by his son Henry. Henry has worked for his father all his life, and has been worrying for some years about the patronising and paternalistic attitude which management have taken towards the workforce. He is also aware that morale among the workers is low. Most people just come in, do the job and go home again, counting the days until Friday and the pay packet. He sees very little sign of people feeling satisfaction with what they do. All the craftsmanship has been taken out of the job – the whole process is done by machine now. Also there is a tradition in the firm of not encouraging social activities directed either by management or by the workers. Old Mr Smasher was a Methodist and a strict teetotaller and would not allow alcohol on the premises. The nearest Smasher and Smasher ever came to a rave-up was when everyone was treated to a glass of orange punch and an individual chocolate swiss roll at Christmas!

Henry is a Christian, and a member of his local Methodist church.

One Sunday a visitor comes to preach at the church. It is none other than Bill, and he tells the congregation all about his work as an industrial chaplain. Henry is impressed by Bill's grasp of industrial problems, and after the service, asks him if he could visit Smasher and Smasher with a view to improving some of the Victorian attitudes and practices in the firm. Bill agrees, and they make a date for his first visit. But before he comes, Bill wants to see some evidence of the problems facing the firm.

Henry has a bright idea. He draws up for Bill two fairly informal profiles of people working for Smasher and Smasher. Here are the documents as Bill received them.

PROFILE 1

NAME Sebastian Norris   AGE 34   POSITION Sales Manager

Sebastian, like the other managers, receives a monthly salary. He has his own office, and a private secretary who brings him tea or coffee whenever he feels the need, and is quite happy to run down to the shops for him or slip his personal letters in for stamping with the company correspondence. The company pays his contribution to BUPA so that were he ill, he could receive private medical treatment immediately. In line with the policy of old Mr Smasher, Sebastian as a member of the management team is also a shareholder, and as such receives a percentage of the firm's profits. If Sebastian needs to arrive late to work because he has to take the children to school, no one makes a fuss so long as he gets the job done. Sebastian has considerable freedom as to how he plans his day. Certain jobs have to be done, but often he can decide on the order in which he does them. Most of the time he makes his own decisions, and only rarely does anyone tell him what to do. Along with the management team Sebastian makes the rules which govern the firm, and which the workers have to abide by. He eats his lunch in the managers' restaurant where the food is served by waitresses. He shares in other managerial perks, such as the ballot for theatre, opera and concert tickets (Smasher and Smasher have a box at the Royal Albert Hall, an annual subscription for six seats in the front stalls at Covent Garden and at the National Theatre).

PROFILE 2

NAME Darren Larkins   AGE 22   POSITION Worker on loading bay.

Darren is paid every Friday, according to the number of hours he has worked. He has to clock in and out of the factory, and if he needs any time off, has to fill in a form and give it to the foreman. The only thing Darren ever sees coming out of Smasher and Smasher are large packing cases with FRAGILE written on them. He doesn't know what is in the cases – and he doesn't care much either. He gets his tea, coffee and lunch in the staff canteen (self-service), and his breaks are carefully timed. He has no choice as to what he does. He simply does the same thing all day. The only person senior to himself whom he sees regularly is the Foreman. Once in a while Sebastian comes to the loading bay for a breath of fresh air. 'How's it going, Darren?' asks Sebastian, for lack of anything better to say. 'OK, Mr Norris', mutters Darren.

If you were Bill, considering the Aims of Industrial Mission and Bill's special interests, what changes might you recommend for young Mr Smasher's consideration?

More problems for Bill

Bill has taken on Smasher and Smasher as a regular concern. He visits the factory on two mornings a week. During one particular week, two problems are brought to his notice.

Grace

Grace Williams is 53 years old. She works on the serving counter in the canteen. Over the past six months she has been off work more than usual and has been frequently late. She has already been given two 'official' warnings about this. Her supervisor in the canteen suspects that Grace is drinking heavily, and also notices small amounts of cash missing from the canteen till. One day, watching Grace carefully, she catches her with her hand in the till. Grace is taken to the Personnel Manager who sacks her on the spot. Grace pleads with him, saying that she is the only person in work in her family, her husband and 20-year-old son being unemployed. When she pleads for one more chance she is told that she's lucky the police haven't been called in. At this point in the proceedings young Mr Smasher hears about it and asks Bill to join in the discussion.

Role play

You will need to get into groups of 5 or 6. Each member of the group should take one of the following characters:
Bill   Henry Smasher   Grace   the canteen supervisor   the Personnel Manager   a shop steward.
(If there are four of you, leave out either Henry or the Personnel Manager.)
  You have a 20-minute meeting, at the end of which some sort of decision has to be made about Grace's future.
(You will need to spend some time thinking individually about your role. What part will you play in the discussion? What will your concerns be? How concerned are you about what happens? Is Grace worth bothering about anyway?)
  After 20 minutes tell the rest of the class:
(a) What decision you reached
(b) Whether it was unanimous
(c) How you reached it.

Sid

Sid has worked with the firm for 25 years. He is one of their leading designers, and his work has always been imaginative and of the highest quality. Recently his friends have noticed that he has become very withdrawn. He has become quiet and morose, and eats a packed lunch in a corner on his own rather than mix with others. His workmates have tried to find out what is wrong, but he won't say. Then one day a colleague hears from Sid's cousin whom he knows vaguely, that Sid's 18-year-old daughter is dying of cancer. The colleague finds Bill and asks him to help.

How might Bill be able to help?

Industrial action

Industrial action may include working to rule or going on strike.

Coursework: Research

Look in the newspapers over the next few weeks and cut out any references you can find about strikes or working to rule. Make a display of your cuttings.

From the cuttings you have found, and from your general knowledge, make a list of the reasons why people strike.

The effect of strikes

Strikes have serious consequences for the worker, the worker's family, the firm, the community, the general public, the economy. Draw six columns in your book, and put one of these headings at the top of each. Working with a partner, write down the effects of a strike on each. Compare your ideas with those of the rest of the class.

Questions for discussion

1 Can a strike ever be justified? If so under what circumstances?
2 Considering what you have learnt about Christian attitudes to the world of work, under what circumstances, if any, do you think a Christian might take strike action?

Unemployment

Group work

In groups, talk about any occasion when you were bored or frustrated because you had nothing to do. How did it make you feel? How did it make you behave towards other people?

Read the following passage by David Eaton.

Worth at work

'Work is a mirror to ourselves. It speaks to us about who we are and what is our worth or value as a human being. This is why the denial of work through unemployment is destructive to personality. For those for whom work has been an important source of affirmation, its removal will seriously threaten the whole self. However much redundancy is tempered by remarks about 'the state of the market' or the 'effects of the recession', it is hard not to believe that it is your worthlessness which has brought about your rejection from the workplace.

Work locks our abilities into an opportunity for their expression. Work allows the creativeness of mind or hand to be released. All can find something of themselves displayed in the work they do and the way they do it. Work reflects back to us the truth about ourselves, who we are and where we stand in relation to other people. The satisfaction of our work will enlarge self or deflate. Work can release yet more ability or stifle what is coming to life. We can feel uplifted by work, or cast down. . . .

Work is also a star by which to fix our position in the community. The rundown of traditional industries has sometimes meant the removal of important stars from the sky. Sometimes their influence has run on from one generation to another; son following father down the pit, or on to the Board. The daily going to the place of work gives a knowledge of who you are and where you belong. Security and wellbeing would be words to use of this experience. It is not unlike the experience Christians have of a church they like, and in which they worship.

David Eaton, *Crucible*, July 1985

Considering what David Eaton says about the importance of employment on a person, discuss what you think the effects of *unemployment* must be. Display your work.

> When a man works he not only alters things and society, he develops himself as well. He learns much, he cultivates his resource, he goes outside himself and beyond himself.
>
> The gravest and bitterest injury of their state (the unemployed) is not the physical grievance of hunger or discomfort . . . it is the physical grievance of being allowed no opportunity of contributing to the general life and welfare of the community.
>
> (William Temple)

Discussion

1   Many people say that everyone has a right to work. What does this mean? What is a 'right'?
2   Do you agree that we all have a right to work?
3   If we do all have a right to work, whose responsibility is it to see that we are all given that right?

> 4   A judge in Northern Ireland reported that a particular area of a city was a breeding ground for alcoholism, drugtaking, violence and vandalism. It was also one of the areas in the UK with the highest unemployment rate. What do you think is the connection between these two statistics?
> 5   Many people believe that it is the loss of an opportunity to be creative and contribute to society which causes many unemployed people to lose their self-esteem. What activities could someone who was unemployed get involved in to help keep their self-respect?
> 6   Many large firms give free counselling sessions to employees who are about to retire – how to cope with retirement. What advice do you think they should give?

The Church and unemployment

The unemployed have no union to plead their cause. The Church should be 'the voice of the voiceless' (John Stott).

The churches in Britain constitute an important pressure group. The churches have money, property and many members in positions of authority and power – such as the Anglican bishops who sit in the House of Lords. The churches also have several millions of members who are also members of society and whose attitudes are important in forming local policy. During the 1980s, as unemployment has spread more than ever since the Second World War, Christian groups have become more involved in helping the unemployed. How can they do this?

A *Changing attitudes*

Many Christians involved with the world of work are beginning to talk about the *new life ethic*. As we have seen, traditional thinking looks at people for what they *do*, not for what they *are*.

The new life ethic
1   Look at the whole person – mind, body and spirit.
2   In a society where money, possessions and economics dominate, we have forgotten that it is human beings who matter.
3   Many people still do boring and monotonous jobs in bad conditions. Isn't it better to have machines and robots doing these jobs?
4   If this happens, more people will be without a paid job. Therefore we must change our attitudes to people who are without a job. They must be allowed to feel that being released from a boring, dangerous or filthy job gives them freedom.
5   We are all dependent on each other.
6   The unemployed have a contribution to make as valuable human beings. They are still people, customers and consumers and as such support economic growth.
7   Only a tiny minority of the unemployed are 'shirkers' who do not want to work.

8   One result of our obsession with money and possessions is that in furthering our economy we are using up the world's resources at an alarming rate. This must change.

9   We need to stop and ask ourselves what we mean by 'the quality of life'. Is this just a matter of the money we have and the goods we possess?

10   Work as paid employment is only a part of life. It does not say all there is to say about a person. Many of the kinds of work people do without pay are more fulfilling and of more value to the community than their paid job. An unemployed person drawing the dole and working voluntarily in a youth club or a home for the elderly, or on a hospital radio must not be thought of as (and must not see him / herself as) 'redundant' or living off the state without making a contribution.

11   Education is important. Schools should not just educate pupils on the assumption that they are going to get a paid job. It is equally important that schools should help pupils to discover and develop their non-academic talents which may lead to fulfilling leisure activities.

B *Projects*
More and more Christian communities are realising that they have at their disposal huge buildings which are rarely used. There is an increasing trend to turn church buildings into Christian centres. Part of the building is used for worship, and the rest is used for weekday projects, some of which involve the unemployed.

At the beginning of the 1980s an organisation was set up called Church Action With the Unemployed (CAWTU).

Moulsham Mill
As part of their attempt to help in the present unemployment situation, some Essex churches formed the Church and Community Interface Association. The purposes of this organisation are:

   (a) to create temporary or permanent work for unemployed people.
   (b) to provide training opportunities for unemployed people
   (c) to look at relationships between: society and the Churches, people of all faiths, the employed and the unemployed, leaders of commerce and industry and trade unions.

The Interface Employment and Training Division is centred on Ilford and Chelmsford, with developments in London, Sheffield, Blackburn, Rawalpindi (Pakistan) and Bombay (India). Unemployed people were consulted about the setting up of the scheme. They said that a programme which gave them even one year's training would improve their chances of getting a job. During the first two years, 1250 people received training, and of these 46 per cent found full-time jobs.

The largest community programme project is at Moulsham Mill in Chelmsford. Thirty people at a time, all of whom had been without

Q&A

WHAT DOES CAWTU DO?

CAWTU creates a resource of information and experience which enables 30,000 local churches of all denominations to respond more effectively to the social tragedy of unemployment. CAWTU provides:

INFORMATION	EXPERTISE	LOCAL SUPPORT	DIRECT AID
A series of leaflets for the specialist worker - Outlines the experience of others, and offers guidance on how to get each type of project started. A directory - Describes 100 projects established under church auspices. A video learning programme - Informs and challenges groups of concerned church people. A newsletter - Supplies news and views on unemployment issues to Friends of CAWTU and to other concerned people.	A National Initiatives Advisor Widely experienced in all aspects of governmental policy on unemployment and available to advise on statutory and other sources of funding for local initiatives. Regional Contact People More than 50; they are mostly industrial chaplains or members of Boards For Social Responsibility. All have extensive knowledge of unemployment initiatives, contacts and networks in their respective localities. A central resource unit A small executive and secretarial staff available for reference, support and assistance as required.	Promotional Assistance CAWTU encourages and facilitates the forming and developing of Local Action Groups. Local Action Groups may affiliate to CAWTU and receive publicity and display material appropriate to their particular tasks. The newly published 'Launchpad' series of leaflets (this is No. 1) is for over-printing, reproduction and distribution by Local Action Groups. Objectives of groups will include encouraging practical local responses to unemployment, learning more about the issues involved and heightening awareness within local churches. Regional Volunteer By meeting the expenses of regional volunteer workers, CAWTU facilitates new local initiatives and research.	Launchpad Grants Subject to fulfilling the necessary requirements, direct grants are made: ● of £200 each to new Mutual Help Groups of unemployed people sponsored by local churches. ● varying between £10 and £200 each to individual longterm unemployed people in selected locations for creative, educational, job-generative or community benefit purposes.

employment for a long time, worked on the restoration of the buildings. The Mill is now the home for nearly thirty small businesses and training workshops. Other activities include self-help groups and voluntary projects.

The Young Workers Project
This project offers training programmes to long-term unemployed people aged between 18 and 25, some of whom are disabled. For example, young people are trained in some of the dying rural crafts, such as glass engraving, candlemaking and pottery. Trainees are also given advice on becoming self-employed and on setting up workers' cooperatives.

Coursework

Knowledge
Find out what the Churches in your area are doing about unemployment. (The Industrial Chaplains' office should be able to help you.)

Understanding
Explain why the Churches are getting involved with unemployment. What does it have to do with Christian teaching?

Evaluation
Either:
Should it be necessary for voluntary organisations like the Churches to run projects for the unemployed? Isn't this the responsibility of the government?
Or:
How successful do you consider the project(s) you studied to be?
Or:
'The Churches have money, buildings and some highly trained and intelligent members. Designing projects for the unemployed is a good way of using these resources.' Discuss.

Prayers

Let us pray. . . .

Lord God, be with our brothers and sisters who are without work.
We ask that they may be given
   – hope in their hopelessness
   – courage instead of fear
   – peace to replace anxiety
   – confidence in place of doubt
   – energy to overcome listlessness
   – and determination which replaces resentment.
Lord, hear us.

May we who have jobs
   – never patronise those without work
   – never write them off
   – never think we are better or more important
   – and never think that material things are more important than people.
Lord, hear us.

Heal our divided nation, Lord, through your Holy Spirit.
Bring together
  – north and south
  – the employed and unemployed
  – the rural and the urban
  – the rich and those on social security.
Bind us together through your love to create a nation worthy of your kingdom.
Lord, hear us.

Lord God, who in Jesus was a friend to those who were cast out by society, hold on to those who feel rejected today. Be with them in their despair, helplessness and fear. That they may come to know you as always present with the victims of the suffering of the world and find hope in you. We ask this through the one who suffered and died, and the power of the One who gives true life to all. Amen.

War and peace

Discussion

1   From your own experience and knowledge, on what sort of occasions and for what reasons would you say people most turn to violence?
2   List the six most common reasons why you think countries go to war. (Ask a historian if you're stuck!) Which of these reasons (if any) do you consider to be just?
3   If there is a major war in your lifetime, which countries do you think would be involved, and what do you think might be the cause? Could there be another way of solving the problem?

Christians in the Armed Forces

This man is not only in the Navy; he is also a Methodist minister. He is known by the men and women of the Royal Navy as 'Padre' – he is a naval chaplain, and holds an officer's rank.

These young men are serving in the armed forces. Yet they are Christians, and are bearing witness to their faith. To some people, being a Christian and doing a job which trains you to kill does not make sense. Others feel, just as strongly, that by serving in the armed forces, and even going to war if necessary, a person is serving his country and could even be said to be keeping the peace.

Nevertheless, as the recruiting pamphlet for Army chaplains points out, the Chaplain is 'totally non-combatant and never carries any kind of weapon'. Forces Chaplains do not see any contradiction between their faith and wearing the uniform of the armed services. They serve people and their needs in the same way as do ordinary parish priests and ministers.

An Army chaplain writes about his experience in the Falklands:

> Before action you go around the trenches talking to people. After action you go to the hospital to see the wounded and pray with them. When the battalion's on the move you stay with the doctors at the Regimental Aid Post but you go up to the front line with the stretcher bearers. You can talk with the wounded and help them not to give up. And of course you take charge of the dead.

It is obvious that not all Christians take the Biblical commandment 'Thou shalt not kill' to include killing in war. In fact the majority of Christians in Europe did fight in the last two wars, with only a handful standing their ground with other pacifists – and being called traitors. For hundreds of years the majority of Christians have accepted the *'just war'* doctrine. This is the belief that some wars can be justified on certain grounds – that there are times when fighting a war is the only way to deal with a situation. The 'justice' of each war must be judged on the following terms:

1   The war must have been declared on the authority of the rightful rulers of the country.
2   The cause must be just.
3   Those who fight must have the right intention, which is, to bring about good and destroy evil.
4   War must be the last resort after all methods of reconciliation have been tried.
5   The good achieved as a result of the war must outweigh the evil which led to the war.
6   There must be a reasonable chance of victory.
7   The war must be fought by proper means. This includes:
  (a) Proportionality – you must use only as much force as is needed in the circumstances, and no more.
  (b) 'The principle of double effect' (the end justifies the means). You may cause undesirable side-effects if the good achieved by action is greater than the evil which would result were no action taken. For instance, the Norwegian Resistance blew up a ferry carrying heavy water for a German reactor, even though this meant the loss of civilian life.

Some very muddled notes!
Form 5G were having a discussion. Sally was away from school that day, and her friend Rebecca tried to help her by scribbling down all the arguments that people raised for or against the issue in question. Unfortunately, Rebecca isn't very good at taking notes. She did not start each new point on a new line, nor did she make a note of whether each argument was for or against the issue. In fact, she even forgot to write down what the issue was that was being discussed!
  Your job is to help Sally sort out Rebecca's notes.

Jesus said 'love your neigbour. It isn't very loving to watch someone being attacked and do nothing about it. But over £100,000,000,000 million a year is spent on weapons. This money could solve the problems of the third world'. Jesus said 'Blessed are the peacemakers' and 'do not kill'. You can't be a Christian AND fight in battles. When your country is at war it is your duty to fight. It is unfair to be pacifist and share in the advantages of a victory you did not help to win. Violence leads to violence. If we show no signs of being aggressive and if we had no weapons no-one would think of attacking us.

People say 'look at the Swiss. They are neutral and in the last war the Germans didn't attack their country. How can you be neutral when 6m Jews are being murdered in concentration camps? Being neutral is like agreeing with it. History has shown that it is the men and women of peace who are remembered with love and admiration. Jesus did not use violence, but that does not mean that we should not. When he said 'turn the other cheek' Jesus meant that individuals should not fight each other. He did not mean that we should not go to war. Peace and love are ideals in the Kingdom of God. We have to live in this world with all its imperfections. Unlike the Kingdom of God, there are evil people in this, and sometimes they can only be stopped by the use of violence.

(a) Read the notes carefully, and decide what issue was being discussed. Think of a suitable title.
(b) Make two columns in your book and head one column 'for' and the other 'against'.
(c) Decide where each argument begins and ends.
(d) Decide whether each argument is for or against the issue.
(e) Taking the arguments 'for', list them in the correct column, starting with the argument which you think is the most powerful, and ending with the weakest. Add any other arguments of your own. Now do the same with the arguments 'against'.

Look up the following passages. What do they tell us about Jesus' attitude towards the use of violence? Do you consider that this teaching should be binding on all Christians today, at all times? Luke 6:27–29; 6:37–38; 22:47–52; Matthew 5:21–24

Pacifism

During the first four hundred years of the Church's history, it was unusual to find Christians in the army. But once Christianity became the official religion of the Roman Empire, it became more acceptable for Christians to fight for the Empire which supported the Church. Just as in the old days, loyalty to the Roman Emperor and the Roman gods were taken to be one and the same thing, so in later times loyalty to God and the King went hand in hand. Yet there have always been Christian groups who have said that to fight, under any circumstances, is totally out of keeping with the teaching of Christ. Jesus said 'Thou shalt not kill', and 'love your enemies'. How then can a Christian ever claim that killing another human being is justifiable in Christian terms?

The Quakers
Perhaps the best-known Christian group who include pacifism in their basic beliefs are the Quakers (The Society of Friends).

The Quaker peace testimony was presented to Charles II in 1660:

> We utterly deny all outward wars and strife, and fighting with outward weapons, for any end, or under any pretence whatsoever; this is our testimony to the whole world. The Spirit of Christ by which we are guided is not changeable, so as once to command us to a thing as evil, and again to move unto it; and we certainly know and testify to the world, that the Spirit of Christ, which leads us into all truth, will never move us to fight a war against any man with outward weapons, neither for the kingdom of Christ, nor for the kingdoms of the world.

More recently, they have said:

> Our renunciation of violence requires a positive effort to encourage and promote non-violent opposition to oppression, which is the only real and lasting means of true liberation. . . . Positive and effective non-violence is the alternative we offer to warfare . . . what price are we prepared to pay for peace?

> (*A Quaker Peace Testimony for Today*, 1978)

Coursework

Knowledge
Find out about the Peace Tax Campaign.

Understanding
Many of the people who belong to the campaign are Christians. In what way have their Christian principles influenced their decision to support the campaign?

Evaluation
Do you think that people can be justified in refusing to pay tax for the manufacture and purchase of arms?

The Church and the Bomb
In 1982, a Church of England commission published a report *The Church and the Bomb*. In this book, two questions are discussed:
1 Can a nuclear war ever be a just war?
2 Is it wrong to possess nuclear weapons?
In answer to the first question, the report concludes that a nuclear war could never be a just war.

Look at the criteria for the just war (p. 174). How do you think the committee argued that a nuclear war could never be a just war?
Most Christians agree with this decision. The Papal Encyclical *Gaudium et Spes* agrees:

Any act of war which aims indiscriminately at the destruction of entire cities or wide areas with their inhabitants, is a crime against God and man, to be firmly and unhesitatingly condemned.

A question which divides Christians firmly into two bodies of opinion is, 'Should a country ever possess nuclear weapons?'
What do you think?
This is a very difficult issue. Here are some thoughts to start you off.

On the possession of nuclear weapons

As possessors of a vast nuclear arsenal, we must also be aware that not only is it wrong to attack civilian populations but it is wrong to threaten to attack them as part of a strategy of deterrence.
(To Live in Christ Jesus, US Catholic bishops)

The possession of tactical nuclear weapons makes smoother the path towards a general nuclear holocaust.
(James McCarthy, a Quaker)

Deterrence, which is the only alternative way of attempting to deal with human conflict, is based on the control of force by so directing its use that its worst effects are prevented.
(Graham Leonard, Bishop of London)

Only by maintaining a credible deterrent is it possible to make nuclear war less likely.
(Gerard Hughes)

On the use of nuclear weapons

It is in this situation, where we might face obliteration as a people, that I would think it permissible to launch a nuclear response, if that response had any hope of preventing obliteration.
(Keith Ward)

Today, the scale and the horror of modern warfare, whether nuclear or not, makes it totally unacceptable as a means of settling differences between nations.
(Pope John Paul II)

On the cost of nuclear weapons

Every gun that is made, every warship launched, every rocket fired, signifies in a final sense, a theft from those who hunger and are not fed, from those who are cold and not clothed.
(President Eisenhower)

Countries squander cash to boost their pride while millions starve. The money spent on arms is scandalous while schools, and homes and hospitals remain unbuilt.
(Populorum Progressio)

On the people behind them

> You can't really think about your future at this age, because who knows what's going to happen and we may not have a future if some kind of war breaks out.

> I wouldn't like to survive because everything else would be gone and you would have nothing to look forward to.

> Older people . . . have them, not us. We don't want them, so if it changed I think it will be someone from our generation. But it's going to take a little while.
>
> (Thoughts of American teenagers)

> A Japanese journalist, Mitsuko Shimomura, reported . . . that American and Russian educators undertook studies to investigate how their own country was introduced in the other's middle school textbooks. The Russian investigators found that the American textbooks presented the Soviet Union as a country that has a one-party dictatorship, that it is expansionist, that it is economically and politically behind the times, and lacks freedom.
> A similarly unbalanced view was echoed in the report of the American team. They found that the Soviet textbooks portrayed America as a country plagued with unemployment, inflation, crime, social injustice and racial discrimination and exhibiting militaristic ambition.
>
> (Nikkyo Niwano, a Buddhist writer)

> . . . and when finally he (the American President) gets away to the golf course . . . at close hand, you may be sure, is that lonely, eerie and ever-present creature who stays never more than ten seconds from the president; the man who carries in his pocket the day's scrambler code that can flash the proper combination to the Red Box nuclear alert system of the Strategic Air Command in the bowels of the earth below Omaha, Nebraska.
>
> (Alistair Cooke, *The Americans*)

Pilgrims of hope at the nuclear air bases
'NO PEACE camp in this village', said the yellow printed notices in the windows of the neat, detached bungalows of Lakenheath.

If this was meant to be a threat it was an idle one, for not more than 50 yards from the last of these notices was the peace camp itself, with 16 caravans and converted vehicles, housing 26 people, seven dogs, and at least one kitten.

The peace campers have been at Lakenheath for two years. Their present site is the fifth they have occupied, and they have been there for a year. In one of the little, cultivated gardens next to the caravans a hen strutted and pecked at the ground.

I found it sad that many of the villagers seemed threatened by such a camp. Why were they not scared instead by the presence of the largest United States Air Force base in Europe, with its 94 F111 nuclear capable fighter bombers?

Did they know, I wondered, that in 1956 Lakenheath, and the surrounding district, came very close to being wiped out when a B47 bomber, loaded with TNT, crashed into a store containing three nuclear bombs?

Yet even such a sobering thought as this must have been far from the minds of the 3000 pilgrims who had marched about seven miles from Mildenhall, the headquarters of the United States Third Air Force in Europe.

It was St George's Day. It was glorious weather. The Red Cross flag of England fluttered on the tower of Lakenheath's ancient church.

At the head of the march Bruce Kent, with a dog on a lead, walked next to Dr Tony Dumper, the Anglican Bishop of Dudley, conspicuous in his purple cassock.

Behind them, an assortment of young families and older people walked alongside a few priests, nuns, and Franciscan friars in their brown habits. Everyone was in holiday mood.

The local people, English and American, were surprisingly friendly. The police were cooperative rather than hostile.

This became evident when they headed off a National Front group with a banner calling for 'No Cruise. No CND.'

The Easter hymns, the peace songs, and the service next to the base all contributed to an atmosphere of Christian hope in the visible face of the nuclear threat.

Catholic Herald, 27 April 1984

Christians for peace

Something to discuss and write about

1   The article refers to Mgr Bruce Kent. Many Roman Catholic leaders felt that Mgr Kent's work with Christian CND was incompatible with his role as a Roman Catholic priest. Try to find out more about this argument, and think about your opinion on the subject.

2   How influential do you think the Churches are in the eyes of Western governments today?

3   Why do you think only one bishop was on the peace march? Do you find this sad, or do you think the bishops did the right thing in staying away?

4   'This is the Easter message.' What do you think Mgr Kent meant on this occasion? (He was referring to the peace march.)

Health and wholeness

John, the hospital chaplain

It has often been said that people find that they need the Church most when they get married, when they have their children baptised, and especially when they are ill, or someone dies.

Why do you think that people might think more about religious questions when they are very ill, or dying?

One group of people who are very aware of this are hospital chaplains – men and women, both ordained and lay, who work full- or part-time in hospitals.

John is a chaplain in a big London hospital. He is a minister in the United Reform Church, and works part-time in the hospital. The hospital has a full-time Anglican chaplain, and part-timers from other denominations. There is one chapel in the hospital where Christians of all denominations worship together.

In some ways, John's job is very much like that of the industrial chaplain. He does not only work with patients, but also with doctors and nurses. Like the industrial chaplain, he is 'neutral', and without medical training. Because of this, he can sometimes help iron out disagreements between hospital staff. 'Young doctors and nurses especially get upset easily because of fatigue and stress. They can shout at me and say anything they want without being afraid that they'll get the sack, or it'll be held against them.'

But most of John's work is with patients. He wears a 'bleep' which can respond to a signal within a 30-mile radius. When it sounds, he knows that he must ring the hospital.

Apart from his routine visits to people on the wards, he may be called when someone is about to die, when a patient is in a panic about what is happening and needs someone apart from a doctor to talk to.

Is life sacred?

The Bible says that human beings were made in the image of God. Christians understand this statement in various ways, but many of them would agree that the human race is very special, and has a special relationship with God.

'Sacred' means holy – that is, consecrated and set apart as being special to God. Many Christians say that human life is sacred. Therefore it must be treated with respect, must not be wasted, and must not be destroyed.

Coursework: Problems for John

Here are some of the problems which John has had to deal with. Working in groups. If you were in his place, what do you think you could do?

Wayne

There has been a road accident as a result of which Wayne, having received serious head injuries, is on a life-support machine. After 45 hours, Wayne is declared brain-dead, and the hospital decides to turn off the life-support machine.

Wayne's mother is distraught, and keeps screaming at the doctors, calling them murderers. John is called in to help.

Alice

Alice is a psychiatric patient about to be discharged. She hasn't a job and needs some money. John is called in to help.

Mabel

Mabel was an old lady. She was a diabetic and lived alone in a house. She could no longer cope with her injections – she kept forgetting – and as a result she was constantly falling down. She was taken into hospital, and the doctors got her sorted out. But then they needed the bed and wanted to discharge her. If she went back home she would only become ill again. John heard about the problem.

Nigel

Nigel is 25 years old. He came to live in London from his home in Liverpool when he was 16. Now he has AIDS. He is dying, and the hospital calls his parents down. They are an elderly old-fashioned couple, and have no idea what is wrong with Nigel. The doctor working with Nigel asks John to advise whether or nor the parents should be told what is wrong with their son.

Reg

Reg is 67 years old. He is dying of cancer, but no one has told him this. Whenever doctors try to open up the subject they find that Reg is very worried about life in general, and they feel that he could not cope with the knowledge that he will soon die. One of the doctors feels very strongly that a person has a right to know when they are dying because they can then prepare for death. He asks John to talk to Reg.

Alison

Alison, aged 7, was rushed into hospital after a serious road accident. The doctors have declared her brain-dead but are keeping her body ventilated by machine. Although her parents are understandably terribly distressed, the doctors need to ask them if they will allow Alison's heart and lungs to be used for transplant. John is called in to help talk to them.

Frank

Frank is 45 years old. He was brought to the hospital six months ago after a fall which smashed his skull. He has been on a life-support machine ever since and has never regained consciousness. The doctors have told his wife that there is nothing more that they can do. He will, in their opinion, never regain consciousness, and is only being kept alive clinically by machines. They feel that the time has come to turn the machine off. She will not accept this. John is called in.

The healing ministry

Jesus told his disciples to preach the Gospel. He also told them to heal the sick. There is certainly evidence in the New Testament that some of the great leaders of the Early Church, such as St Paul, had the gift of healing. Also throughout history, a few 'saintly' people have been said to have this power – people like St Francis. One of the conditions for being canonised (made a saint) in the Roman Catholic Church is that at least one miracle has been performed as a result of prayers being said to that person.

It is only in recent years that the whole Church has begun to take seriously Jesus' command to 'heal the sick' as applying to *all* Christians. Is it only 'saints' – very special people – who have the power of healing? Or is this power at the fingertips of all Christians? In answering this question, Christians have also begun to ask what exactly we mean by 'healing'.

The Church's Council for Health and Healing

The CCHH was set up in 1956 by Archbishop William Temple. The Council concentrates on five aims:

1 To rediscover the healing ministry in all the Churches, and enable it to grow and develop.

2 To forward cooperation between religion and medicine.

3 To provide resources from which people can learn about the Christian healing ministry.

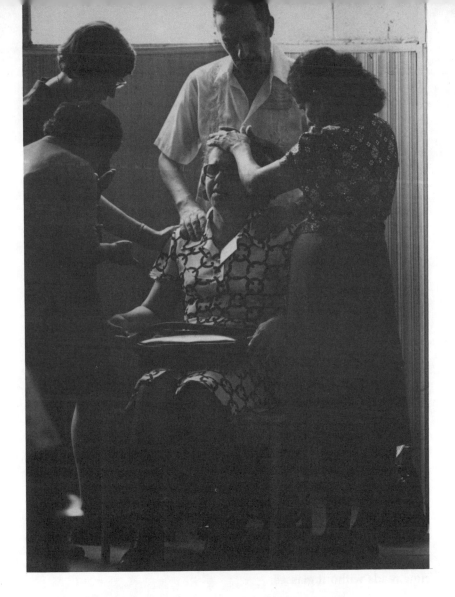

4 To provide training in the Christian healing ministry.

5 To encourage study about the healing ministry.

There are representatives of 23 Christian denominations on the Council. (The Roman Catholic and Pentecostal Churches act as observers but do join in activities.) Also the Royal Colleges of Medicine, Nursing, Dentistry, etc. are represented. The Council now has its centre at Marylebone Parish Church in London, in a newly-converted crypt.

The Christian healing ministry is *not* primarily concerned with 'miracles', or 'faith healing' as many people call it. Christian healers believe that there is far more to 'healing' than just the cure of physical ailments. Instead, the ministry is concerned with *wholeness*. It sees healing as directed to all aspects of the person – physical, mental, emotional and spiritual, and regards all forms of healing as gifts of the Spirit. So, in St Marylebone Church, you would find (among others), a GP's practice, a pastoral centre, dealing with counselling and healing, a scanner, acupuncturists, osteopaths, music therapists, and the Samaritans. On the first Sunday of each month there is a service in the Church above during which the 'laying on of hands' is given to those who wish to receive it.

Christian healing recognises that there are often very close links between physical ailments and emotional/psychological/spiritual problems. Most doctors recognise stress and anxiety as causes of many illnesses. This is why Christian healing is concerned with the *whole* person, not just with curing physical problems.

That is not to say that 'miracles' or 'divine surprises' as the healing ministry might call them, do not happen. It has been recognised for a long time that some people do have a special gift for actually curing people. The CCHH has made a teaching and discussion video. On this film, two people talk about their experience of being not only healed but also cured.

Russell

Russell lost 46 per cent of his sight when a photocopier exploded in his face. The consultant who treated him said that he had a 1 in 25 chance of his vision improving over the next 20 years. Then one day, a Methodist minister phoned Russell and told him that his congregation had prayed about him, and wanted him to go and see a man at the Pin Mill Fellowship who would lay hands on him. Russell went to Pin Mill. As hands were laid on his head and over his eyes, Russell says that he experienced a 'blue colour', and a gentle electric current passing from the hands through his skull and body. A right hand was placed at the back of Russell's head and the left hand over his left eye. Russell says that he felt something pass between the hands. As a result, his eyesight was restored, and he now reads without glasses.

Carolyn

Carolyn suffered from multiple sclerosis. She was young, and not surprisingly felt anger and resentment at being confined to a wheelchair. She also felt a great need to experience God's forgiveness, and one day went to a healing service. During the service, the minister asked that anyone who needed praying for should stand up. Once more Carolyn felt resentment creeping through her. How could she stand up? At the end of the service, the minister came to talk to her and listened to her moans and groans. Why were some people healed and others not, she wanted to know. In the end the minister asked if she would like him to pray with her. She said yes. Then, for the first time in two years she felt her feet tingling, and felt an urgent need to stand up. She stood, and walked to the back of the Church with a rather worried minister calling after her, 'Do be careful.' Yet Carolyn says that the most important thing to her was not the cure of her body but the way she felt 'healed' inside.

Lin

Lin Derreck was born with cerebral palsy, and early attempts to treat it left her partially sighted. Her parents refused to give up, sending her for physiotherapy, until at the age of 13 she walked her first steps. Then just as things seemed to be looking up, at the age of 14 Lynn lost the use of her one good eye, and this led to both her eyes being removed. Typical of attitudes at the time, the Education Authority wanted to put her in a school for educationally subnormal children because of her double handicap, even though she was a perfectly intelligent young woman. Instead she went to a school for the blind where she gained 3 O-levels and also passed flute exams. She went on to work as a telephonist at a city bank, eventually being put in charge of training all new telephonists.

Lin will never be cured. She is totally blind and in a wheelchair. Yet she highlights another aspect of the CCHH's work – coming to terms with disability and illness. She has not only come to terms with physical disability, but has turned it to advantage. She has taken counselling training and is a Methodist lay preacher. She has also written her autobiography. Lin regards her blindness as a positive advantage in her counselling work, for she is never prejudiced by first impressions of what people look like. Lin specialises in bereavement counselling, and says that the loss of her eyes was not dissimilar to the loss of a friend or relative. Similarly her inability to walk enables her to get closer to people who are aware that she needs their support as much as they need hers. She also counsels handicapped people going into residential care units, and can discuss their problems from personal experience. Lin regards herself as more 'whole' than she was, and recalls the words of Jesus in the Garden of Gethsemane, 'not my will but thine be done'. 'All the best things have happened to me since I lost my sight', she says.

Another point of view

Not all Christians are so convinced about the value of the healing ministry. Some would go so far as to describe those involved in the ministry as 'cranks'. In an interview with John Mortimer, David Jenkins, Bishop of Durham said that

> concentrating on the miraculous sidetracks people. It encourages them to believe in all sorts of things like spiritual healing. And then miraculous claims put ordinary, sensible people off Christianity. They say 'tell it to the Marines' and so they miss a great opportunity for good.
>
> (*Sunday Times*, 12 April 1985)

Activity – group discussion

1   Do you know of any cases where stress, anxiety or depression has brought on physical illness? (Try not to give the names of people you know during your discussion.)

2   Do you believe that people can be cured in the way described by Carolyn?

3   If this sort of cure does take place, how do you think it happens?

4   If this sort of cure does take place, why do you think some people can be cured but not others?

5   If you were very ill, do you think you would go to a healing service? If so, what would you expect to get out of it?

6   When Carolyn said she felt 'healed inside', what do you think she meant?

7   What qualities do you think Lin has which make her such a good counsellor?

8   What do you think Lin means when she says that she is now 'more whole' than she was?

9   Lin said that all the best things had happened to her since she lost her eyes. She is able to regard her disabilities as a positive benefit. Can you think of any other ways in which we can learn from suffering?

10   In her story, Lin makes it clear that her parents worked very hard to help her achieve what she has. If you were Lin's parent, what do you think your feelings would be about her now?

11   If it were possible to detect disability such as Lin's while a baby was in the womb, many people would say that it should be aborted. Do you think that the lives of people like Lin have any bearing on the abortion argument? Discuss your views.

12   Look at what the Bishop of Durham says. Do you agree with him that 'miraculous claims' put sensible people off Christianity? If so, why should this be?

7 What next?

The world is changing fast, and the Church is changing with it. Every year brings new discoveries, new problems, new questions to be answered, and very often these questions challenge the traditional beliefs of Christianity as expressed in the creeds.

Check your understanding – Group work

Read again the creeds on pp. 24–5. Using the index of this book, and other resources available to you, discuss with your group, and make notes on Christian beliefs about:
1 God
2 Jesus
3 The Holy Spirit
4 The Bible
5 The Church
6 Forgiveness and reconciliation
7 Death.

Questions for discussion – Group work

A Discuss in your groups what you think should distinguish a Christian from other people.
B What do you think Christianity has to offer the world as we approach the year 2000?
C Do you think there are any advantages, in a changing world, of having religious faiths which change very little, keeping their traditions and their beliefs? If so, what might these advantages be?
D Do you think that the Church must change if it is to attract and be of service to people in the future? If so, in what ways?

To change or not to change?

We began this book by looking at the denominations within Christianity. Each of these groups has its own leadership and has certain beliefs and practices which distinguish it from others. We have also seen how some of these groups have attempted to reunite, and how other attempts at unity have failed. Over the past 100 years, a new type of division has appeared in the Church. This division is not necessarily related to the well-known denominations, but rather cuts across them. Many people today see the main division within the Church not as one among Catholics, Orthodox, Methodists, Baptists, etc.; but between 'traditionalists' and 'radicals'. The traditionalists of every denomination want the teachings, customs and values of their

Church to remain unchanged. The radicals believe that the Church must change with the times, and say that some of the teachings, now 2000 years old, are out of date and need to be redefined.

Questions for discussion – Group work

Make two lists, one headed 'traditionalist', and one headed 'radical'. Write down any Christian attitudes, activities or beliefs which you think come under each heading. (For instance, think of attitudes towards the Bible, Church, or morality.)

Face to faith

In the 1960s John Robinson, Bishop of Woolwich, wrote a book called *Honest to God*. In this book he aired his doubts about subjects like the Virgin Birth and the physical resurrection of Jesus. Many Christians were angry, saying that a bishop's job was to defend the faith, not question it.

In the 1980s David Jenkins, Bishop of Durham, has done much the same thing. He too has said publicly that not all Christians, and not all priests and bishops, believe in the traditional teachings of the Church. He also raised again the question of whether the Church should become involved with politics, and was himself very outspoken against Mrs Thatcher's government. Many people said he should resign, but others agreed with him.

Questions for discussion

Read carefully the following extract from an article written in the *Guardian's* 'Face to Faith' column by John Gummer in April 1985. He was then the Chairman of the Conservative Party.

Also read the letters to the *Guardian* written in response to the article. Then answer the questions on p.190.

I have no doubt at all of the right and the duty of the Church to speak out on political matters. Indeed, people are wholly mistaken and unable to understand what the Church is about if they believe that the Church should say nothing about politics at all. If we believe that God created the world and that He was incarnate – God made man – then we are denying the Creator and the Incarnation if the Church is not concerned with every aspect of life and human endeavour. Politics – particularly in the Western tradition – encompasses a good deal of life.

As a practising Christian and a politician, I am confronted with the constant problem of facing the demands of the Gospel in the exercise of my daily work. It is for the Church to remind me of those demands and through the sacraments dispense the grace to live up to them. But it cannot give me the answers to political questions any more than it can tell the carpenter what style of chair will sell best or prove most comfortable.

For the Church to enter into the political arena it must be sure it is speaking for Christ and not merely promoting a particular point of view – right or left.

Lastly, there is Christian certainty. Bishops and church leaders must avoid making statements which are merely matters of opinion. The fact that the recently retired Bishop of Peterborough made political statements which appeared to support the Conservative Government detracts from the universality of his statements on matters theological. I happen to agree with his views on politics but I would prefer him not to say them lest they diminish the effect of his preaching the Gospel.

Bishops whose party political views grab the headlines often find it much more difficult to reach the heart of the people on matters of faith.

Sir, – There is a sweet reasonableness about John Gummer (Face to Faith, April 29) that disarms criticism, but the numerous questions which his article manifestly begs demand a reply.

He concedes the right of the Church to speak on political issues but suggests that this right belongs primarily to bishops – many would incline to the belief that God is less selective in making His will known.

Mr Gummer was, no doubt, correct to deny bishops the right to pontificate on economics – in a science as abstruse as theology itself politicians and even economists might abdicate that right – but this argument must not be used to silence the Church when it pinpoints policies which ignore the need for a "bias to the poor" or which treat workers as a commodity and not as persons.

As chairman of the Conservative Party Mr Gummer has a right to explain the ways of politics to his fellow Churchmen. He has also a duty to explain the ways of the Church to his fellow party members.

Did he explain to the Prime Minister why the Church was unwilling to follow her blueprint for the service in St Paul's after the Falklands War?

Sir, – Mr Gummer's Face to Faith article is remarkable for its naivete and poor logic.

The fact that a bishop does not have an expert knowledge of, say, transport policy does not mean that he should not speak up. He has at least two valid reasons for doing so. First, a bishop serves a region and the interests of regions vary enormously. The effects of the Government's transport policy will be very different in Tyneside – in Bishop Jenkin's diocese – from their effect in Suffolk.

More fundamentally, if bishops feel that the interests of some classes, some areas, some ethnic groups are being unjustly neglected or attacked, it is their clear Christian duty to say so. The Bible gives no clear guidance on transport policy, pit closures or monetarism but it does give clear guidance about the need for compassion and to treat all human beings with the respect they are entitled to as part of God's creation.

Finally, and perhaps most important, Mr Gummer urges churchmen to desist from speaking about issues which are "merely matters of opinion." This would debar them from all debate about the values we should be pursuing, both individually and collectively.

I would not for a moment wish to argue that the moral and social teachings of Christianity can or should be identified with any one political ideology. However, they do provide a series of precepts to which all politicians must give heed regardless of their ideologies or party allegiance.

Mrs Thatcher and the Bishops

Mrs Thatcher has urged Britain's bishops to preach a moral revolution, it was revealed yesterday.

She invited top churchmen to Chequers and asked them to stop dabbling in politics and spend more time trying to raise standards of decency.

The Prime Minister called the meeting because of her deep concern that the Church was not giving a moral lead to the nation, particularly to young people.

She told the Archbishop of Canterbury, Dr Robert Runcie, and seven other bishops that she wanted to secure a new partnership between Church and Government for a drive to bring back traditional morality.

It was a message hammered home by Home Secretary Douglas Hurd, who told a fringe meeting at last week's General Synod: 'What society most desperately needs from the churches today is a clear, definite and repeated statement on personal morality.'

Mrs Thatcher's meeting with the bishops happened at Chequers last November, but only emerged yesterday.

The Bishop of Oxford, the Rt Rev Richard Harries, who was there said: 'The Church has been in the business of calling on people to assume moral responsibility for their own lives for nearly 2000 years. It will still be doing that 100 years hence, long after the Government is gone and forgotten.'

Mrs Thatcher will encourage her ministers to keep up their pressure on the Church in speeches.

Daily Express

1 (a) What do you think the Government in 1988 regarded as 'traditional morality'?

(b) Make a list of things which you believe the Government wanted the Churches to teach, under the heading of 'Raising standards of personal morality'.

(c) Do you think it is the Government's responsibility to tell the Church of England what it should be teaching? Does your answer apply to other Churches as well?

2 (a) List ten things which your group considers to be most important, under the heading of 'Personal morality'.

(b) Do you think that these things are largely absent in our society and so need bringing back? If so, whose responsibility is it to see that these standards are introduced?

(c) In what ways, if any, do you think the Churches can work to improve 'moral standards'? Does 'raising moral standards' mean, for instance, telling people what they should or should not be doing?

3 In another statement, the Home Secretary also suggested that schools had lost their control of the young, and were also responsible for the nation's moral decline.

In what ways can schools help young people develop their own code of moral behaviour? Is it the responsibility of schools to do this?

4 The article stresses the need for the young to receive moral teaching.

Giving reasons for your answer, say whether you think young people need a 'moral lead' any more than older people.

5 Do you think it is true that most people want the Churches to give a strong 'moral lead'?

6 The article stresses that the Church should be teaching traditional morality and the gospel rather than dabbling in politics.

Are the two activities incompatible?

Write down a list of things which are political and also moral or Biblical issues (e.g. trade with South Africa, war). Are there any issues which politicians are concerned with which are *not* moral issues?

These may be some of the answers – but what were the questions?

This book has attempted to look at some of the answers given by Christians to certain questions which seem to be common to the experience of the human race.

Hans Küng, referring to the writings of the philosopher Immanuel Kant, gives a list of what he calls 'ultimate . . . perennial questions of human life.' Read these questions and discuss the questions that follow.

What can we know?

Why is there anything at all?

Why not nothing?

Where do we come from, and where do we go to?

What is the ultimate reason and meaning of all reality?

What ought we to do?
Why do we do what we do?
What deserves forthright contempt, and what love?
What is the point of loyalty and friendship, but also what is the point of suffering and sin?
What may we hope?
Why are we here?
What is there left for us: death, making everything pointless at the end?

1 What is an 'ultimate question?' Can you think of any others?
2 What answers do you think Christians might give to Küng's questions?
3 What answers do you and your friends give to these questions?

Index